On Dying and Denying
A Psychiatric Study of Terminality

Gerontology Series

Sheldon R. Roen, Ph.D., Series Editor

On Dying and Denying
A Psychiatric Study of Terminality

Avery D. Weisman, M.D.

Department of Psychiatry, Massachusetts General Hospital
and Harvard Medical School, Boston, Massachusetts

Foreword by Herman Feifel, Ph.D.

Behavioral Publications, Inc.   **New York**
1972

Library of Congress Catalog Card Number   79-174268
Standard Book Number   87705-068-6
Copyright © 1972 by Behavioral Publications, Inc.

BEHAVIORAL PUBLICATIONS, INC. 2852 Broadway
Morningside Heights, New York, New York 10025

Printed in the United States of America

In the glittering shallows of time run currents, passing quietly, protesting, yet flowing. Realities fated not to be happen in their own stillness. But then the impossible itself becomes: verdant leaves lie wounded, dry up, and blow away. The river and the rain wash the earth and sky together, drift downward to the sea.

Polyphemus

Contents

Foreword

Mid-twentieth century man is highly uncomfortable in confronting personal death. Man of the Middle Ages had his eschatology and the sacred time of eternity. Along with judgment came the possibility of atonement and salvation. And, more recently, modern temporal man lived with the transformation of the promise of personal immortality into concern for historical immortality and for the welfare of posterity. Even this is no longer vouchsafed. The modern age, as Hans Morgenthau has noted, threatens not only the individuality of death but social immortality as well, in its capacity for making both society and history impossible. An era of dissolving beliefs and traditions is despoiling conceptual creeds and communal relationships which, heretofore, permitted us to transcend and integrate personal death. In a society that emphasizes the future, the prospect of no future at all is an abomination. Hence dying and death invite our hostility, repudiation and denial, and assume taboo status.

American culture, confronting death, has attempted to cope by disguising it, pretending that it is not a basic condition of all life. The health professional responsible for care of the dying has also been captured by this orientation. His training emphasizes healing and the extension of life and therein he secures his emotional and financial rewards. When efforts to forestall the dying process fail, the health professional usually loses interest and transfers his motivation and resources elsewhere. Professional knowledge is used as a buckler against unprotected encounter with death. Even when dying is observed, it is customarily viewed through a screen of technical functions—logged lungs, distended livers, faltering hearts, but rarely as a human experience. Our institutional structures which deal with dying appear to be more organized to meet anxieties and requirements of the treaters and living than genuine needs of the dying. The unhappy result all too often is that the dying patient is left to die emotionally and spiritually alone. We do not even permit him to say goodbye.

Nevertheless, robust denial of death is becoming increasingly difficult to sustain in a world of multiplying violence, potential nuclear holocaust, and freeways. Further, recent advances in medical technology (organ transplantation, hemodialysis, etc.) altering the character and duration of dying, and expanding recognition of the mental hygienic value of open communication concerning dying and death with the fatally ill person are beginning to brush aside existing curtains of silence.

Dr. Weisman is one of the foremost explorers of how people meet the threat and challenge of impending death. Although sensitive to scientific canon and to demands of the scientific enterprise, he has not allowed himself to become bewitched by methodology and analysis at the expense of purposive meaning and illuminative value. He discerns the limitations of applying a mathematical physics model to experiencing man and sidesteps a scientism which "excludes human and personal elements." In the book, he employs his rich clinical experience and intellectual acumen to delineate the manifold patterns of denial, in subterranean guise as well as in surface manifestation, related to dying and death. He views denial as a total process and specifies how it can serve to negate reality and also to nullify threat in order to help one participate in reality. He instructs us how diagnosis of denial in disease and dying too frequently rests on partialities and reality standards of the examiner, with neglect of the patient's perception of the world. Finally, he quickens our appreciation that the essence of dying extends beyond biology and is a psychosocial role as well as a physiological event.

Dr. Weisman has looked deeply and understandingly into the heartland of human nature as it grapples with oncoming personal extinction. He articulates a perspective and provides us with guidelines which point the way toward "better" and more "appropriate" dying. As future dying patients, we are all in his debt.

Herman Feifel, Ph.D.

Los Angeles, California
March, 1971

Preface

This book was at least six years old when it was rewritten still another time. Of course, it had not yet been published, but chapters had been torn out, amplified with details, extended with fresh data, and then revised in different versions for special occasions. Consequently, although the original purpose has not changed, the perspective has. How people meet the threat and challenge of impending and inevitable death is substantially influenced by their observers and survivors, who tend to interpret terminal events according to their own dispositions and prejudices. The psychiatric physician who studies death and dying becomes a participant who cannot preserve uniform objectivity under all circumstances. Were such objectivity possible, however, the essential empathic encounter would be forfeited. The mutual experience of facing death with a person whose extinction is imminent is an illuminating and instructive endeavor; to disregard the investigator's personal perspective and evolving philosophy would, therefore, distort the validity of his conclusions.

Originally, Dr. Thomas Hackett and I planned to report our

findings jointly. We had collaborated on a project, *Death and the denial of death,* as we had on prior investigations. Unfortunately, our clinical activities and interests have diverged so much in recent years that co-authorship proved impracticable. We agreed, however, that as principal investigator, I should continue to compile our data and to carry out the presentation. The case histories and basic viewpoint are the result of our collaboration; the responsibility for much of the theory is mine. I cannot share the blame for whatever imprecision, inaccuracies, and unacceptable inferences have crept into the work. But I hope, as will others, that in time Dr. Hackett will present another version of the extraordinarily rich material that we were privileged to study together.

In the past decade, thanatology—the secular study of death and life-threatening behavior—has become almost a subspecialty of psychiatry. From what I can gather, it has already become a branch of social psychology and anthropology. Books and articles, for both the layman and professional, have rapidly accumulated. Doctoral theses have been written about the psychology of death. Journals and learned societies have been established to encourage further scientific and cultural studies. Nevertheless, despite the delay in finally presenting our material, no detailed study of death in its specific relation to denial has yet appeared. Instead, the process of denial is still discussed as if it were an independent, unambiguous, self-contained mental mechanism that everyone understood. While the study of denial as a psychodynamic process is common enough in psychiatric literature, its configurations with respect to death have not been explored.

Most of our clinical material came from patients at the Massachusetts General Hospital, where the close association of treatment and research has been traditional. As a result, we had an unusual opportunity both to investigate the course of fatal illnesses and to follow afflicted patients under different types of circumstances.

Distance encourages perspective, but with the passage of time, the immediacy of certain clinical material tends to trickle away. The critical problem has been to preserve a balance, precarious though it is, between scientific documentation and existential reality. Mere numbers of patients cannot guarantee scientific validity, nor can mere numbers of interviews with comparatively few patients assure reliability. Solemn scientism dictates that only uniform methods and comparison groups be used. This is seldom possible in work that depends upon assessment of subjective states. There is a hazard, of course, in reporting words and events that cannot be replicated. But it is hazardous only from the viewpoint of experimental science. Clinical investigation of how people feel and think when faced with their own death cannot be experimentally simulated. Furthermore, were we to reduce dying patients to their least common behavioral denominator, their individuality would be the first factor to be eliminated. A dying person is not a dead body, nor is dying simply an anonymous end-point. Without strategic emphasis upon the subjective elements in death, the study of dying would be devoid of humanity.

The problems of the dying patient are as diversified as the problems of the living patient and of being alive. The so-called "problem of death" is mainly problematic because we have not fully appreciated that our own psychological reticence and revulsion have prevented asking appropriate questions. We have been disposed to accept easy consolation and time-honored denial of death. Scientism, after all, may be a disguise that denial dons to mitigate the impact of personal extinction. The fact of death is an answer to all our questions. The equally pervasive process of denial may insist that only a thoroughly objective assessment can be acceptable, especially if pre-existing dogmas so decree. The problems inherent to death are only special cases of problems presented by life that we have little hope of encompassing fully by scientific means alone. Less formal methods of inquiry protect the immediacy and imagery of death; more intellectualized appraisals can be built upon suitable concepts and theories that emerge from the actual encounters with death. Only the fact of death is final; everything else is uncertain and inconclusive. Dogmatic contradictions and overly general concepts probably stem from the soil of denial.

Physicians try to outwit and to reach a compromise with death, but they cannot eliminate it. Medicine is a science of death; to anyone who understands its protean shapes, death permeates the substance of life. Death is already here; it is within the gates, dogging our footsteps, echoing our voices, and constraining most of what we do. When we seek to deny, mitigate, or transform the sounds and sights of death into more congenial and compatible forms, we usually end up out-witting life itself.

The key to philosophical analysis is to know when to stop philosophizing. The purpose of the psychological study of death is to know when to begin philosophizing. When we work within a field we are already pressing beyond it. Consequently, psychiatric investigation is not restricted to the analysis of verbal events and compelling anecdotes. Psychological factors are central issues in the management of terminal patients. Patients consult doctors because of sickness; doctors can offer diagnosis and treatment. For the terminal patient, however, the less tangible elements of care and safe conduct until death are no less important. The practical significance of mortality forces physicians to transcend traditional boundaries and professional preoccupations. Psychiatry enables a doctor to learn how his own denial works; even though they may have signed innumerable death certificates, most physicians have concealed themselves from the death within.

Support for *Death and the denial of death* came from the Foundations Fund for Research in Psychiatry (62-247). During part of this period, I was also Consultant to the Project on Old Age and Death, Cushing Hospital, Framingham, Massachusetts. The resources that helped bring this book to an appropriate conclusion were provided by the Center for Studies of Suicide Prevention, National Institute of Mental Health. As principal investigator of "Project Omega," a psychological autopsy study of preterminal illness and suicide (MH 15903), I have had additional opportunity to study other cases of threatened and incipient deaths.

I wish it were possible to acknowledge my individual indebtedness to colleagues and associates who have contributed so much support, cooperation, and clarity through the past few years. To name some of these people would certainly cause the risk of overlooking others. There must be something about working so close to death and to ultimate situations that reduces many of the frictions usually found in professional endeavors. I have found both friendship and challenge in this work. This I can attribute only to the generosity, forebearance, and perspective that day-by-day confrontation with death evokes.

A. D. W.

Project Omega
Boston, Massachusetts
February 25, 1971

1

The Practical Significance
of Mortality

The prospect of death bewilders modern man no less than it did his preliterate and superstitious forebears. Despite revolutionary changes in our style of life brought about by technological innovations, people still face personal death with dread. Education, hyperliteracy, world-wide communication, and daily confrontations with wars and other tragedies have not accustomed man to death. Despite the magnitude of impersonal deaths, and despite man's seeming sophistication, his moralistic platitudes, and familiar mythologies, he is frightened to death by the specter of death. New eras have produced only newer versions of ageless conflicts. To the mystery of why we are born to die there have been, and still are, only two solutions: Death is either an idealized extension of terrestrial life as we know it, or it is simply complete and unambiguous extinction.

It is a tragic irony that we can now prolong lives and spare thousands who might once have perished, only to discover newer and more drastic threats to human existence. In the

Middle Ages, war and disease decimated populations, infant mortality was rampant, and medicine was little more than witchcraft and tradition. The hazards of being alive were so great that death and salvation were almost synonymous. Indeed, death itself was a gateway to either paradise or perpetual damnation. In any case, it had a meaning that seemed to justify the precarious prologue called life.

In our secular age, we are not so sure that death promises redemptive release. Lifton (1967) reported that for some Hiroshima survivors, life became saturated with the imagery of death. Frankl (1963) told us about the limitless brutality of death camps in which death was such an everyday banality that it became far less frightening and painful than did the indignity and meaninglessness of prolonged survival. Niederland (1961, 1968) has shown that certain concentration camp survivors suffer from a seeming inability to die, and therefore are condemned to endure a fate more distressing than that of those who succumbed.

Most people today have no deep convictions about life after death. Nevertheless, secularization of life has not made death more acceptable or less terrifying. These are curious findings. If death is not meant to vindicate life, and if life is not a preparation for death, as earlier ages professed, why is death still an alarming idea? In the past few decades, scientific interest in the psychology and sociology of death has increased. Perhaps this has occurred because we have become more aware of the paradox between extended life expectancy and the glowering threat of obliteration (Weisman, 1967). Earlier in this century, Sir William Osler (1904) was one of the few prominent physicians to show any professional interest in the human significance of death and dying. Today, however, publications dealing with topics such as bereavement, violence, mourning, fatal illness, panic states, and life-death crises have become so abundant that even specialists cannot read them all.

Of course, death has always been a favorite theme in art and literature, ranking just below love and sex as one of the predominant interests of man. Most people respond with tingling fascination to stories of crime and catastrophes, perhaps as a result of having escaped a similar fate. Whether we have escaped being a victim or a perpetrator, and which alternative offers more satisfaction, is a matter of conjecture. Nevertheless, despite man's preoccupation with death and dying, whether in romantic novels or philosophical treatises, these wise and appealing messages are unimportant to the individual who is, in fact, about to die, or who has suffered the loss of a loved one.

Scientific study of disease and what people die from is a product of modern times. To prevent and postpone death we must know the causes and circumstances of disease, especially as it affects the organism. Until very recently, however, we have not heeded all the factors that can influence or undermine survival. Humanistic and psychosocial research has lagged far behind purely biological studies. Yet, our gathering interest in the psychology and sociology of death (Fulton, 1965) insists that we should no longer take survival for granted. Even the stark impersonality of death in our age forces us to reconsider the special values of human life. If man is so fragile, vulnerable, and transient, what can it mean, after all, to be alive?

The secular study of death recognizes that the traditional answers of religion to the problem of death are inconsistent and unsatisfactory (Herberg, 1958). If death is not an automatic refutation and mockery of whatever we have lived for, what is its significance for man? The distinction between the quick and the dead is unambiguous enough. Nevertheless, there are conditions in which man is half-alive or half-dead, depending upon our preference, and still other circumstances in which life and death seem to be reversed, and all meaning of the distinction is lost.

How shall we learn how people come to terms with imminent death? If we can discover more significant and more acceptable ways of facing death, then perhaps we will also find a method of accentuating the values and goals of life. This aim is the "practical significance of mortality."

PRACTICAL PROBLEMS IN DEATH

To answer simple questions complicated studies are sometimes required. Practical problems often need to be formulated from a global perspective in order to be more specific. For example, to understand what any man goes through in facing his own death, we must realize that, singly and collectively, man is perpetually engaged in an oscillation between coming-to-be and passing-away. In the crucible of time, he is a mindless thing reacting to forces beyond comprehension. Yet, from the inner viewpoint of his own perceptions, each man believes in his total responsibility and in his capacity to choose and control many of the events that befall him. Sometimes he feels free to select the degree of his own freedom, so that he is not at fault for his misfortunes. He can think, feel, and do; he can examine his own vulnerability while assuming his endurance. In the midst of his self-congratulation about the gift of consciousness, it is abidingly true that he is born to die, his reality is evanescent, his season is brief, his existence is fragile, and his span of survival dubious.

The theme of death is built into our institutions and culture (Blauner, 1966). For example, it has been said that without hope of immortality there would be no religion, and that without dread of death and retribution there could be no laws or concept of personal responsibility. These ponderous propositions, fortunately, are largely peripheral to the practical concerns of a physician. However, even the most practical medical specialist is a product of his culture, community, prejudices, and personal dispositions, all of which are derived from ages past and from his own antecedents.

One of the most pervasive qualities of death in practically every culture is that it is taboo or forbidden (Rivers, 1926). In order to approach and touch dead things or things that have been touched by death, we insist upon special rites, formulas, and even select certain members of society to take our place and to argue our case with lethal forces (Eliade, 1964). Ceremonies and rituals are strategies that are intended to mute, mollify, explain, or redirect the elemental threat implied by death. There is a primitive parallel between our apprehension about a menacing situation and our conciliatory euphemisms used to describe it (Gorer, 1956). In the very beginning, man devised legends and myths to explain why and how death first came to man and walked upon the earth. Usually these myths reported that a titanic struggle had occurred long ago, and that death was the result of a loss, never a triumph (Abrahamsson, 1951). Customs and creeds always preserve a discreet and sanctified and euphemistic distance from death. Secular and religious tactics pertaining to death share a common intent: to placate an adversary.

Because the realm of death has been forbidden, objective investigation has been fragmentary. As a result, many contemporary attitudes toward death are almost identical with the ideas held by primitive man. In his classical description of primitive thought, Werner (1957) emphasized the confluence of action and emotion, what one does becomes identical with what one feels. Names, things, events are not distinctive, but rather different properties belonging to a single occasion that is lived through and experienced, and not merely perceived as something with an independent existence in the outside world. Primitive thinking persists in us all to some degree, even among those who pride themselves on their intellectual sophistication and sober objectivity. The imagery and metaphors of death become less personal as civilization becomes more complex, but death is still, today as much as long ago, an elemental and ineffable event that can only be understood according to the prevailing legends of our day. For most people, death is a fateful and regrettable necessity. Yet, they harbor a primitive belief that appeal is possible, that suitable negotiation is available, and that, granted the forebearance of adversaries, death might not, after all, be compulsory.

But we must ask again: If death is a natural outcome of life, why is it universally regarded as an evil? If this belief were not axiomatic, there would be no need for fanciful traditions and elaborate rationalizations to conceal the enormities and dreads implicit in death. Each society differs in its strategies for controlling and negotiating with death. Some groups believe that death is the penalty for violating a natural law. In this way death is not wholly adventitious. In other societies, certain people are selected to be trained and to petition for the souls of the dead. The Shaman refuses to accept the finality of death and is prepared even to visit the Beyond in order to effect a rescue or release. In our modern society, there are also people who are educated and equipped to intercede on our behalf. If they cannot forestall death, then they are expected to relieve our anguish. Our practitioners, priests and physicians, are skilled in facing death on its own terms. It is not, therefore, surprising that doctors and clergymen are endowed with reverence and fear. Death contains elements of both the sacred and the sinister; anything or anyone associated with it acquires something of its taboo and special awe (Frazer, 1923). Like death, the victim is often thought to cause still further deaths and to permeate other kinds of human contact. Death, disease, corruption, sin, and error tend to flow together and to create an untouchable symbol of life's negation. Doctors and priests are also somewhat untouchable because they are intermediaries between this world and the next. The respect that physicians and clergymen receive is, of course, an uneasy ambivalence; our society respects them, not for their skill in curing or consoling, but because they are familiar with deadly forces.

The practical problems of mortality are based upon the legendary forces perpetuated by myths and upon the relics of magic in modern life. An earlier age accepted that one should acquire the craft of dying in order to insure an appropriate death (Comper, 1917). Rituals, rites of passage, and suitable responses guaranteed both the serenity of survivors and, presumably, the souls of the deceased. Even among skeptics, today's funeral is an efficient format for parting company with the dead.

The funeral is an occasion for remembrance and for closure. It is a descendent of more primitive and arcane rites that placated evil spirits, because to die without reverence and to be interred anonymously are as objectionable and fearful today as to die and to be unburied were to ancient Greeks.

Despite our reverence and fear of death, death is often dehumanized. There are penalties and laws against mutilating or desecrating a dead body. But to ignore the person who is dying, as happens in many institutions, is also a kind of mutilation and desecration of the dignity in death. As far as I know, this type of dehumanized treatment is without penalties.

WHAT DOES DEATH MEAN?

Pronouncements about the "meaning" of death are usually platitudes, enabling the speaker to voice his own prejudices and preconceptions. Every individual dies to his own life; what his passing signifies to his survivors is apt to change. For almost everyone, however, the meaning of death is that it is a *universal negative*, repudiating and nullifying the objectives so sought in life. Sometimes death is said to be a "blessing" because it affords timely relief from suffering, but this is not a primary value. Given a choice, healthy people would opt for a timely death that shortened suffering, because death is thought to be destructive of pain, as well as of everything else.

According to most scales of value, death is scarcely an estimable, worthwhile objective. It has far too many negative results to rate very high. It separates people, deprives one person of another, inflicts misery upon the least deserving, and dispenses an unremitting degree of evil. It is an enemy readily personified, even though it gets at us in many different ways, through injury, illness, catastrophe, failure, humiliation, and defeat.

Despite the invincibility of death, we still harbor a belief that it could be resisted and cajoled, were we wise or prudent enough to take necessary precautions. Because we have no idea of just what steps to take, death merges with decay and destruction of all kinds. More precisely, death, decay, disease, and destruction seem to emerge from a common source. Our boundless ambivalence allows us to offer consolation to the bereaved, and by helping them tolerate their loss with fortitude, we also strengthen them against fear of the dead body and of the ghost. Death is an inverted image of life and vitality; because he represents such an evil force, the dying person may himself be shunned, patronized, or otherwise dealt with according to the ancient, benumbing rituals of conciliation and repulsion.

PURPOSE OF THE BOOK

Very little is known about how ordinary people adapt to the personal reality of their own death. It is not unusual to find hospital charts filled with details about laboratory tests and physical abnormalities, yet without any comment about the patient's thoughts and feelings. Although disease is only one possible explanation of sickness, and there are many sicknesses that result in death, medicine usually makes no allowance for the psychological and social components of mortality.

How do people resolve the crisis of dying? Is denial an effective strategy? How do patients facing certain death manage to live with this knowledge? Is there a "will to live" that can be called upon at critical moments? Can hope be sustained without unrealistic reliance upon denial? What makes for a good death, as contrasted with one filled with anguish, despair, and confusion? How can physicians, as well as others who tend the dying, help dying patients to prepare for death with dignity?

These are a few of the difficult questions asked in this book. The strategy of avoidance and denial, induced by a tradition of magical and dogmatic preconceptions, has not provided adequate protection for the dying and their survivors. Its principal effect has been to segregate the dying and to create an atmosphere of hearty and false innocence about a basic fact of existence. Death and denial are the themes of this book because most adults cannot imagine facing death with clarity, equanimity, and acceptance. Despite the propinquity of death in everyday life, many adults have never witnessed a death, never attended a funeral, or been in contact with anyone who is acutely bereaved. Death is simply not real.

Tactics that deny death are like the pious fictions that we once used to discourage children from asking too many questions about sex and birth. Now, of course, adults do not hesitate to answer questions that only a few years ago could not have been asked. No longer is the tendency to "protect" children from uncomfortable facts so widespread. We realize now that the paradoxical outcome of such protection was, often enough, to bring about the very problems that deception and denial were supposed to prevent.

Since questions about birth now receive a more rational hearing, can we ask honest questions and make dispassionate judgments about that other existential frontier, death? This book is intended to move in that direction. Our questions, therefore, should be phrased in the language of clinical experience and of understanding how people actually undergo the terminal phase of life.

Just as innocence is not the same as ignorance, knowledge about death in the abstract differs from actual contact with dying people. Although the study on which this book is based was limited to hospital patients, its purpose has been to find general principles. To do so, we could not merely be physicians studying disease, nor psychiatrists dwelling exclusively upon vicissitudes of emotion and conflict. The proper balance between empathy and objectivity is admittedly difficult to achieve, and we may not have been successful in every case. It is easy, for example, to be objective when attending seminars on the cause of crime. But if we return home and find that a burglar has ransacked our house and destroyed our prized possessions, it would be less than natural not to feel outraged and bereft. So, too, if we exchange our professional impersonality for the surrogate grief that a genuine survivor or dying patient must feel, this would be no more useful. In the presence of calamity, we can allow ourselves to feel outrage, grief, or indignation, but only insofar as we can maintain compassionate objectivity. Otherwise, we run the risk of imposing our own configurations of denial and self-deception.

Problems about death are neither as abstract as philosophy pretends, as theoretical as religion professes, nor as grim and uncompromising as our portent of global holocaust. Secular death is not always synonymous with a universal negative, nor must it be a symbol of every deplorable quality found in life. Ordinary deaths of ordinary people are seldom very dramatic. Yet, everyday observations and mundane, but compassionate inquiry may disclose how these people manage their deaths and what it means to die. Of course, such inquiries are not casual; they are products of tenacity, self-awareness, and willingness to recognize different varieties of denial.

Death has an admitted fear and fascination for everyone. We are not exceptions. But the first step in overcoming fear of ghosts is to stand firm and not to run away. One looks into the darkness, experiencing fear, but then looking into the causes of that fear. Surrounded by cultural aversions and precepts that urge us to be conciliatory towards forces that are stronger than we, it was possible to shun the easy answers and, for the most part, to recognize and disavow denial. My objective has been to understand more about the reality of death and to find the practical significance of mortality.

2

Basic Concepts and Assumptions

There are many beliefs, theories, and myths about death that seem to persist from one generation to the next. Some beliefs, of course, can be widely held, without being correct, while other ideas may be correct, without being very basic. The difference between a so-called "basic concept" and a "misconception" is often the difference between our own assumptions and the other person's prejudices.

It would be pretentious to claim that every belief about death can be traced to a finite number of concepts and assumptions. However, most discussions about death seem to be based upon four types of assumptions. In this sense, the concepts derived from these basic assumptions can be described in the following ways: (a) the primary paradox, (b) fear of dying and fear of death, (c) talking about death, and (d) hope and the acceptance of death.

12

THE PRIMARY PARADOX

The primary paradox is that while man recognizes that death is universal, he cannot imagine his own death. The belief is illogical, but persistent, and should not be thought of as a mere word game. The primary paradox points up how death and denial are fused from the beginning. It is a real paradox, not the result of consciousness being unable to conceive of its negation (Freud, 1925).

It is other people who die. When man grieves, it is because he has lost someone significant to him, not because their death foreshadows his own. True enough, few people state candidly that they will never die. Even the most fundamentalist person finds it difficult to declare that he will continue to exist in his present form for all eternity. Nevertheless, there are people who do behave as if personal death had little reality, and that reprieve from obligatory death might be possible.

The primary paradox produces many conflicting attitudes. Death may be thought of merely as a remote possibility, or as a necessity bearing little threat. There is nothing absolute about our knowledge of death. Largely, it is a universal phobia that man tends to believe can be avoided, and avoided again, until, for all he knows, it might be postponed indefinitely.

The penalty we pay for believing that death comes only to other people is that it takes us by surprise. Ill-prepared, we then face impending extinction with bewilderment, anguish, and whatever denial can be mustered. Inner convictions are actually the product of opposing beliefs, only one of which manages to reach consciousness at any one time. Our principles result as much from paradox as from clear perception. It is painful to face the world without someone we have loved, but it is almost impossible to foresee a world without our presence. We create the world by putting together whatever we feel to be real. How then can we imagine a world without being alive to experience it? The primary paradox reflects our uncertainty about how this world can be separated from our own sense of self.

FEAR OF DYING AND FEAR OF DEATH

The primary paradox can be resolved, but not until we can understand more about *annihilation anxiety*. This is an unfamiliar term for a familiar sensation. Its companion concept is *alienation anxiety*, dread of being cut off from sources of our own reality and of our significance. Annihilation anxiety, however, means a dread of complete extinction, anxiety about becoming nothing at all. It is based, however, upon two very common ideas which are often confused with each other. These are the *fear of dying* and the *fear of death*.

Fear of dying and fear of death seldom afflict people who are face-to-face with literal death. Instead, they occur most often and to varying degrees throughout life. Fear of dying is a state of episodic alarm, panic, turmoil. It is associated with excessive autonomic symptoms, and usually conveys a preemptive conviction that collapse is at hand. When the fear of dying is intense, reality testing abandons the hapless victim. Familiar cues that indicate a stable world are no longer there. Ordinary objects and events seem strange and threatening; the world, literally, is about to disintegrate. All that is left is an empty feeling of being bereft, confused, alone. Patients may reel, or clutch at themselves with terror, as if to hang onto some stable ground. They grab at objects, at thoughts, at mere words just to keep from slipping into oblivion and anonymity.

We need not go into the comparative merits of different theories of anxiety. Most students make a distinction between "primary anxiety" and the "secondary anxiety" found in phobic reactions and traumatic neuroses. Schur (1953, 1958), who represents the traditional psychoanalytic viewpoint, believed that the prototype of primary anxiety is to be found in the child's fear of falling or of being deserted. Rheingold (1967), however, described a similar cluster of anxiety symptoms that he called the "catastrophic death complex." In his opinion, dread of death is brought about by the unconscious hostility that a mother feels toward her child. May (1950) has presented still another interpretation of "existential anxiety."

Fear of dying is seldom, if ever, fatal; it rarely presages death. Why then, we must ask, is the phrase, fear of dying, so commonly heard? I suggest that it is a metaphor that expresses a condition of reality which brings together a highly personal event, imminent annihilation, with a primitive dread that mankind has always reserved for that most ultimate event, his own death.

Fear of death is not an immediate event, but rather a reflection about man's helplessness. It is a prominent symptom in hypochondriasis, masochistic characters, and obsessional states. As a rule, fears about death are much stronger than the evidence produced by actual disease and invalidism. In fact, chronic fear of death is often represented by nagging thoughts about unrealistic disasters about to occur. "What if this or that catastrophe struck . . . what if that car had hit me . . . what if this cup of coffee contained poison . . . what if I were struck by lightning . . . ." These distressing ideas may actually sustain people and be a distinctive quality of life; they are neither preludes to extinction nor omens of tragedy about to take place. Similarly, for some people, incessant boredom or persistent detachment from reality may be in response to chronic fears about death. There is no *precise* thought corresponding to the fear of death, and it seldom is accompanied by autonomic symptoms. Fears about death are composite fears generated by wistful lack of meaning and motivation. We become lonely, disappointed, alienated, or else we belabor ourselves with tedium and a sense of unremitting sinfulness. In short, fear of death is a basic concept because it seems to regard Death, capitalized to indicate its personal menace, as the embodiment of every form of human evil, failure, disgrace, disaster, and corruption.

TALKING ABOUT DEATH

It is almost impossible to speak about death and dying spontaneously. Annihilation anxiety coupled with denial casts a cloak of mystery over our existence, so that we mistake the primary paradox for our natural state of being. When faced with a dying person or with someone who is bereaved, we become acutely embarrassed, "mortified," and cannot talk about death without guilt and anxiety.

Our reluctance to speak about death is only partially explained by our sensitivity, sympathy, and compassion. Werner and others have demonstrated that words have a primitive equivalence with the underlying reality to which they allude. Therefore, to speak about real death, as opposed to death in the abstract, puts us in the role of someone who violates a taboo, a situation in which there is little distinction between a violator and a perpetrator.

More practically, in the hospital, when a patient is found to have a serious, life-threatening illness, the first question asked by solicitous families and friends is whether to tell. As a rule, their decision is not to tell. "Personally, I would want to know, Doctor. But after all he's been through, he might get too upset, and I just couldn't face it!" These are not frivolous or selfish objections, because families, like anyone else, suffer from shock, threatened bereavement, and repercussions of ambivalences. The guilt that often makes people feel like accomplices is not the same as the unconscious desire to inflict harm. Guilt may arise from sincere regret that they have not been able to avoid a calamity and to prevent death. For this reason, families and friends may want to avoid the implicit reproach that mere confrontation with the victim might elicit.

To tell or not to tell is seldom an urgent question (Weisman, 1967). Contrary to popular expectations, to be informed about a diagnosis, especially a serious diagnosis, is to be fortified, not undermined. In any case, patients soon are aware that something is amiss, and that their closest relatives and friends are poor actors. Ineffective treatments, persistent symptoms, and slippery responses to questions reveal the true state of things long before the doctor and family get around to talking about the diagnosis, and, if necessary, death. By this time, of course, talking about death is no longer a significant issue.

Only in the area of pediatrics and terminal illness is it customary to ask responsible family members to decide for the patient. Were we to act in accordance with what we profess about psychological processes, we would *first* tell an adult about the diagnosis and plan for treatment. Only then would the doctor, after consultation with his patient, decide what and when to tell the family.

Admittedly, it is a painful process when we elect to talk about death and to acknowledge that the reality of death is very concrete, indeed. Custom and compassion mistakenly lead to a conspiracy of silence, denial, and dissimulation. Even though the motives of silence and denial are authentic enough, there is a risk that dissimulation will widen the gap between patient, family, and physician. Barriers increase; disinclination and fear of death may terminate with a paralysis of action. At the end, there is no provision for constructive management of social, physical, and personal complications of terminal illness.

The topic, talking about death, concerns not mere activity, but is the product of basic concepts and assumptions about death. Until we can accept the personal reality of death as a common legacy of mankind, of mine as well as yours, pertaining to me as well as to that other person, we will remain caught in a dense web of artifice and denial. When we can truly accept our own mortality, the primary paradox will not be quite so perplexing. Natural awareness of our mortality will make us less disingenuous, less guilty, and less fearful in the presence of someone else's truth. Truth is not so bitter that it always must be downed in a single gulp, nor is it so poisonous that we must avoid it completely. Truth, like medicine, can be intelligently used, respecting its potential to help and to hurt. The principal worth in sharing truth is to encourage viable responsiveness between people as long as possible.

After we come to terms with talking about death, details such as what to tell, when to tell, how much to tell, and how often and in what form it may be repeated can be arranged for the needs of the individual patient and the compunctions of the survivors. It is as dogmatic and inexcusable to insist upon full disclosure about a deadly disease early in the course as it would be to proscribe any discussion whatsoever.

The manner of disclosing information about a fatal illness cannot be cast in rigid formulas. We can be sure, however, that even scientifically trained patients, such as an afflicted doctor or nurse, are not very concerned about technical details. Physicians who talk to patients as if they were conducting ward rounds are often annoyed and puzzled when their careful comments seemingly are unheard. It is not that patients are obtuse; their central concern is not the scientific fact of having a disease, but rather the question of whether their doctor cares enough to be accessible. If a patient asks, "What do I have?" he usually means, "Can I count on you?"

Crude confrontation, pseudo-objectivity, and hypocritical denial are not the only alternatives in talking about death (Litin, Rynearson, & Hallenbech, 1960). It is hard to "break the news." Preparation is required both for the sake of the patient and that of the doctor. One physician, rightly admired for his knowledge and dedication, always preferred that his cancer patients find out about themselves from someone else. One day, however, he did pause to speak gently with a man who was obviously deteriorating. The patient asked a few questions that the doctor answered with reasonable candor. On the following day, the patient asked another question that was much more direct, implying that he had not absorbed the conversation of the day before. To the shock and surprise of everyone, the physician's tactful manner exploded into anger, "Damn it, man, you've got cancer! Don't you at least understand that?"

HOPE AND THE ACCEPTANCE OF DEATH

If death were, in reality, the uncompromising evil that we assume it to be, and had merely to be endured, without appeal, there would be little reason to pretend that dying people could be helped. We would be stung into silence, and from a distance, we would fend off communication with militant denial.

Perhaps death does make us mindful of our powerlessness. Acceptance, however, is not synonymous with capitulation. In many instances, patients have little choice but to make the best of a very bad situation. But the bad situation may be the worst of a preventable plight. It is possible to countermand despair, not by fortifying denial, but by transcending denial and by respecting mutual autonomy and whatever measure of freedom remains.

People without hope see no end to their suffering, whether or not they are suffering from a fatal illness. Hope, however, is not dependent upon survival alone; survival can be the "No Exit" reason for losing hope, not for preserving it. Hope means that we have confidence in the *desirability* of survival. It arises from a desirable self-image, healthy self-esteem, and belief in our ability to exert a degree of influence on the world surrounding us. Of course, hope does not require absolute control, or no one would be hopeful. It does demand conviction that we can change the world a little bit. Absolute hope is as fictitious as absolute despair, and perhaps as futile. The significant difference between authentic hope as an animal process that spontaneously claims authenticity, and hope as a futile gesture against overwhelming suffering, is the difference between a healthy act, called hoping, and a vain pursuit of unattainable objects.

Hope is decided more by self-acceptance than by objects sought and by impractical aspirations. Indeed, patients facing imminent death are usually far less hopeless than are psychiatric patients. Foreshortened life does not in itself create hopelessness. No one accepts death, impairment of self-esteem, and physical deterioration with good grace. But this may not be undermined wholly by knowing that we are very sick and may not recover. More important is our belief that we do something worth doing, and that others think so, too. Thus, people lose hope when they are unable to act on their own behalf and must also relinquish their claims upon others.

Glaser and Strauss (1968) described how death requires a series of social readjustments, called a "status passage." Others have recognized that dying itself is a social process, not very dissimilar from other kinds of life crises. It is not unnatural for certain adjustments and accommodations that the dying person himself is left out. As a result, isolation may aggravate suffering and disability simply because the patient is called upon to endure more. Finitude is not the same as futility. Few patients readily admit that reprieve is beyond reach, but most are helped by sharing what they do, in fact, know. One woman patient, suffering from cancer of the bowel, came to dread the daily visits of her doctor. She candidly realized that it was harder for him than for her to stand at the entrance to the room, feeling unable to do or say anything helpful as her life dwindled away. To make him feel better, she minimized complaints, spoke optimistically, and attempted to foster denial in her doctor! This turn of events was possible for her only because she had a close friend with whom she could discuss the gathering problems of dying and being dead. Ironically, her doctor's inability to face death provided her with an opportunity to stay alive as a person because she continued to help him as long as possible.

Hope and acceptance of death are basic concepts because they insist that mortality is a dimension of living, not merely a negation or an end-point that cancels out everything. Hope is, indeed, the basic assumption in living and dying, and it sickens in an atmosphere of persistent, ill-founded deception and denial.

Dying people are often hopeless. But diminished self-esteem and utter impoverishment within a painful present can make helpless invalids of us all at any time. We do not need a false dream to protect our animal hope. A solution that simple would demean our dignity as human beings. Survival for the sake of longevity alone is scarcely worth the price. One man who realized he was being kept alive only because of frequent blood transfusions and round-the-clock nursing care, concluded one day that to continue was not worth the effort. "How can I make bargains?" he said, "Even if I could go on, I still say, No!" Note that he did not declare that he was not worth keeping alive. He meant that, for him, survival was no longer necessary.

The crucial issue is between survival and significant survival. Mere survival because of longevity, however brief, is determined merely by how long vital organs can be stimulated and prodded. Significant survival is more personal than that of viable organs. Authentic hope is nourished by healthy animal function, but it is sustained by respect for the person who must die. Hope and acceptance of death are natural accompaniments of each other. The inescapable fact of death belongs to the incomprehensible act of being alive. The living need the dying as the dying need the living, for the same reasons. If we accept being alive, then we must accept the fact of death.

3

Common Misconceptions
about Death and Denial

Except for the finality of death itself, we can point to few
absolute truths—or fallacies, for that matter. Our truths are
largely relative and approximate. They are determined by the
observer, the conditions of his observations, the circumstances in which he finds himself, and, not the least, the
predispositions and prejudices that slant his perceptions.

A "misconception" is an incorrect belief, regardless of why
we believe it. Some people do the right thing for the wrong
reason; others do the wrong thing, despite knowing better.
They may be charged with following misconceptions, either
because they believe what is incorrect or have carried out an
incorrect idea.

Everyone has misgivings and qualms about death, including
professionals who preside at different stages of the dying
process. Personal dread and antipathy may interfere with full
comprehension of dying. Many facile generalities are misconceptions masquerading as axiomatic principles (Weisman,
1970).

Under certain circumstances, almost any proposition or principle or procedure may be defended. Misconceptions, however, are usually declared with such certainty and confidence that it is difficult to find the contingencies that qualify their truth. In contrast, correct principles are true only to a point. Their limited scope is not concealed beneath false generalities.

There are many misconceptions about death and dying people. I have selected a few to discuss in this chapter because they are both widespread and global in scope. In fact, as a rule, misconceptions reveal themselves by being presented almost as exceptionless verities that scarcely anyone would or should question. Some misconceptions have a central truth that has been obscured by unwarranted extensions and applications; others have acquired secondary meanings that inadvertently mislead and do not explain.

THE WILL TO LIVE AND THE WISH TO DIE

Wanting to live and wishing to die are not true opposites. In suicide, for example, it is not unusual for a person to put his life in jeopardy in order to register a protest or to correct a painful element of his life. He expects to live, despite the suicide attempt, and in some cases, specifically because the suicide attempt will correct what he has not been able to change by other means.

The "will to live" and the "wish to die" are cant phrases frequently used by people looking after and upon the dying patient. We cannot be sure what these expressions mean. If sick patients tend to speak up firmly, or show a brave front in the face of distress, the staff often concludes that such patients have a strong will to live. On the other hand, if sick patients seem sluggishly indifferent, or make no secret of their distress, observers infer that these people have a wish to die that cannot be denied.

Assigning motives to people on the basis of flimsy evidence is always precarious. Ready generalizations about another person's "will" and "wishes" are apt to be extensions of our admiration or criticism. The hypothetical strength or weakness of will to live and wish to die, in most cases, is a measure of our moral judgment, not of our clinical acumen.

It is easy to generalize and oversimplify matters of life and death, especially when they concern someone else. When healthy people are asked what they would do, should they be found- to have an incurable illness, many promptly declare that they would commit suicide. Actually, evidence indicates that suicide is rather infrequent among cancer patients. But the initial thrust of the healthy person's response is that he would exercise an option: the so-called will to live would be replaced by a wish to die. The option of suicide is, for some people, a "viable alternative" to the prospect of future disability and suffering associated with incurable disease and dying. Their misconception emphasizes how difficult it is for a healthy person to imagine willingness to die, short of suicide, and how unthinkable it is to put themselves in the place of a dying patient who accepts death without wanting to die.

The intention to take one's own life rather than to submit to a fatal illness is rarely implemented (Farberow, 1962). Cancer patients, for example, may attempt suicide, but not simply because they have a serious, life-threatening disease. As a rule, it is the threatening disruption of personal relationships that prompts a cancer patient to attempt suicide, just as it does with other people. A statistical survey (Campbell, 1966) showed that suicide occurs frequently among patients who have cancer involving the head and neck, when compared with cancer elsewhere in the body. If we accept the accuracy of these findings, we are still curious as to whether these lesions are operable or not, and whether the suicide occurred late or early in the course of illness. We can imagine the plight of patients with cancer around the head and neck. The lesions rarely can be concealed. Mutilation, deformity, disability, and pain are frequent consequences of treatment. Carcinoma of the larynx, for instance, can be treated by surgical removal. The patient becomes mute, and without extensive training, he is condemned to a silence that is almost synonymous with alienation. In some respects, the work and family life of laryngectomized patients may be more drastically affected than if they had died. Furthermore, men with tumors around the head and neck may be relatively young, and sometimes have growing families. Thus, the threatened psychosocial deformity may be too much to bear, and suicide follows. The wish to die seems a better solution to the difficulties posed by the will to live.

According to Menninger's (1938) famous triad of deadly wishes, the wish to die is closely allied with the wish to kill and the wish to be killed. In other words, the wish to die can be more readily understood as equivalent to a wish to destroy or be destroyed, rather than as the antithesis of the will to live. Indeed, the wish to die has many meanings besides that of destruction. It may represent an avowal of a love beyond life, or almost anything that confers a deep sense of commitment.

Even in terminal illness, the wish to die and the will to live have different meanings. If, for example, the image of extinction fuses with fantasies of being reunited with a lost love, or if death is associated with manifest heroism that magnifies self-esteem, such as dying for a cause, then the wish to die and the will to live become identical.

It has become a commonplace to call people who use drugs and alcohol "chronic suicides." Although excessive use of drugs and alcohol may be life-threatening, their purpose is to blunt the painful impact of reality, not to die. Drugs and alcohol revise reality as it is lived. People may be victimized by the side-effects of such remedies, but the primary wish to destroy may be directed at outside reality, not towards themselves. It is not the specter of death that evokes misery, as a rule, but the prospect of endless, meaningless existence. Disability, deterioration, diminished worth afflict and extinguish far more people than does incurable disease.

There is a difference between the "will to live" as an inner experience and the will to live as a hypothetical function. Wishing and fearing, attractions and repulsions, appetites and aversions belong to human intentionality. The will to live is an expression of hope coupled with a sense of effort. It is a belief that obstacles and impediments can be overcome or at least changed for the better. From the inside, the will to live is synonymous with living and becoming. If it becomes associated with the human process of dying, then the will to live is not necessarily a misconception, but a quality of life when faced with an ultimate situation.

There is also a difference between the "wish to die" and passive acquiescence to the inevitable. The wish to die may indicate hope for a future in which effortless death brings relief and resolution.

Consequently, although generalities about the will to live and the wish to die are misconceptions, careful consideration of what each means shows that they are not antithetical, but rather *two versions of hope*, the organic drive to survive as long and as well as possible. It is the prejudiced observer who insists that there is a sharp distinction between a laudable will to live and a deplorable wish to die. In this way, he protects himself against annihilation anxiety. He tells us little about how people die, but more about how he would like the world to be.

COMMON FALLACIES ABOUT DYING PATIENTS

The plight of the dying awakens every man's sense of dread and annihilation. Yet, as Swift said, "It is impossible that anything so natural, so necessary, and so universal as death, should ever have been designed by providence as an evil to mankind." Nevertheless, our common belief, augmented by cultural bias, is that death is a deplorable, evil, unnecessary, and premature event. Death is encased by custom. Our rituals, formal and spontaneous, reflect an enormous concern about being in the presence of the dying and the soon-to-be dead.

In this section, I use the physician as the prototype for anyone who is forced to consider the interface between life and death. As a professional, however, the physician influences the way that other people approach death. Because dying people are simply living people who have reached an ultimate stage, the doctor's misconceptions may distort their image of death.

Medicine is only partially scientific. Much of what a practitioner does depends upon empirical procedures, ethical precepts, sanctioned mythology, and much, much magic. Were any doctor to depend wholly upon scientific knowledge, he would be as constrained and disabled as anyone who could act only upon proven principles: He would be lost and ineffectual.

To be a responsive and responsible physician is almost an impossible profession, in the presence of incurable disease and dying. Just at the time when a doctor needs his skill and knowledge, they fail him, out of the nature of things. He is forced to improvise, and at times, his art becomes artifice.

Fortunately, patients tend to endow physicians with the aura of the priest and medicine man, both of whom can perform magic. The advantage of magic over science is that it does not need to be true. Magic and sorcery have nothing to do with truth and proof. They are strategies for dealing with special beliefs about reality. Medical practice draws upon folk-wisdom, and it is as indebted to folk-fallacies as to folk-truths. In the realm of death and dying, magical formulas and incantations frequently pass as principles. Consequently, physicians can readily, even inadvertently, call upon their prejudices and act upon preconceptions. As a result, fallacies about dying patients may be perpetuated from one generation to the next, insulated by a tradition that exempts these beliefs from investigation.

Here are a few typical, widespread fallacies about the dying:

1. Only suicidal and psychotic people are willing to die. Even when death is inevitable, no one wants to die.
2. Fear of death is the most natural and basic fear of man. The closer he comes to death, the more intense the fear becomes.
3. Reconciliation with death and preparation for death are impossible. Therefore, say as little as possible to dying people, turn their questions aside, and use any means to deny, dissimulate, and avoid open confrontation.
4. Dying people do not really want to know what the future holds. Otherwise, they would ask more questions. To force a discussion or to insist upon unwelcome information is risky. The patient might lose all hope. He might commit suicide, become very depressed, or even die more quickly.
5. After speaking with family members, the doctor should treat the patient as long as possible. Then, when further benefit seems unlikely, the patient should be left alone, except for relieving pain. He will then withdraw, die in peace, without further disturbance and anguish.
6. It is reckless, if not downright cruel, to inflict unnecessary suffering upon the patient or his family. The patient is doomed; nothing can really make any difference. Survivors should accept the futility, but realize that they will get over the loss.

7. Physicians can deal with all phases of the dying process because of their scientific training and clinical experience. The emotional and psychological sides of dying are vastly overemphasized. Consultation with psychiatrists and social workers is unnecessary. The clergy might be called upon, but only because death is near. The doctor has no further obligation after the patient's death.

Fallacies lead physicians into inconsistencies, and into judgments that confuse the clinical with the moralistic. Precepts help to rationalize assumptions and to shelter the doctor from undue anxiety. Assumptions, particularly false assumptions, decide conclusions in advance. For example, these seven fallacies are, in effect, tacit justifications for not getting involved with death. Were the physician openly to confess his reluctance, he might paraphrase the fallacies like this: "Anyone who is willing to die must be out of his mind. Death is a dreadful business, because I am afraid of dying. I have done everything for this patient that I know. I wish I could do more. I don't want to be blamed, but I can't stand being around anyone who is going to die, especially if I know him. Even though we all know what is going to happen, let's pretend that all is well or soon will be. Maybe he doesn't know, after all. He hasn't ever asked me about his sickness, and certainly never mentioned dying. If he suspects, and he may, I suppose he would rather not know. Leave well enough alone. If we did force him to talk about the future, maybe he'd be more discouraged, or even take matters into his own hands. The family is pretty helpless, too, but I'll make sure that his pain is under control. Why did that family think I was going to upset him when we first found out what was wrong? We've never mentioned it, so far as I can tell. Now, the best thing to do is keep him comfortable, let him die in peace. We don't want to make anyone suffer unnecessarily. The facts are there, but it will do no good to dwell on death. The family seems to be taking it pretty well, but they'll get over it, they always do. Nature will take its course, if things can just be kept quiet. I don't need a psychiatrist to tell me what I know already. When the time comes, I'll ask the family minister to get in on this and offer some consolation. He'll be taking over soon, anyway!"

Dying patients who are attended by physicians who feel this way are probably fortunate. The scene is sympathetic, compared with the bleak prospect of dying alone and unattended. My point, however, is not to argue the merits of one kind of doctor as opposed to the management of another. Compassion and concern are in this mythical doctor's words, but the management he advocates is primarily intended to comfort and console himself.

Only someone who is extremely apprehensive himself would fail to see that many dying patients accept death with equanimity and without mental disturbance. To regard acceptance of death as a sign of being suicidal or psychotic amounts to believing that anyone who attempts suicide is insane and, therefore, beyond help, just as psychotics are beyond help—egregious fallacies, all.

To be more specific about these seven fallacies: the first three rationalize withdrawal and establish more distance between doctor and patient. The fourth fallacy infers that the patient is also disinclined to talk about death. Unwise confrontation is, by definition, apt to cause mental disturbance. We cannot assume, as this doctor does, that someone who asks no questions has no questions to ask. He may have no opportunity to ask, or he may be afraid to ask, lest he repel people on whom he depends. Families cannot decide judiciously about what to tell. They rely upon the expert for advice and can be swayed according to the doctor's beliefs. The fifth and sixth fallacies presuppose that when the patient is not regarded as responsible, with eyes to see and ears to hear, his silence is assumed to mean that he is both ignorant and complacent. Withdrawal does not necessarily mean serenity, nor is open accessibility equivalent to inflicting "unnecessary suffering." It is commonly heard that physicians do not talk about death with very sick patients in order to keep up their hope. But they usually add that the patients are probably already aware of their condition, and so do not need to be told! If there are rationalizations ready for any contingency, how can anyone be wrong?

Let us continue: survivors do not always get over a serious loss and return to "normal," without first suffering a great deal. Sometimes, bereavement leads to serious somatic and psychological symptoms during the next year or two (Parkes, 1970). Mourners may become patients. Yet, some doctors continue to believe that anticipatory bereavement is peripheral to more genuine medical concerns.

What is "unnecessary suffering," that is, so often, cited as a reason for nonintervention? Who is to judge what varieties of suffering are necessary or not? Whose suffering are we concerned about? During the terminal phase, not many patients ask for miracles, only for evidence of care and concern.

The most damaging and lethal fallacy in this, as in most other situations, is that of stereotyping people and problems. When we categorize anyone, doctor or patient, we reduce them to a least common denominator, and they become less than what they are or could be. The alternative, then, is to look for the exceptions, and meanwhile, to treat everyone as a special case.

PREDILECTION AND PURPOSEFUL DEATH

The most tenacious, invidious misconception is that death and fear are inseparable. Some clinicians go so far as to assert that anyone who fails to show pronounced anxiety is denying fear of death (Sheps, 1957). This is a tendentious fallacy. The doctor finds a patient who seems relatively calm, even though he is facing death. He then concludes that "denial" is the reason for the equanimity! Without conceding that harmonious acceptance of death without denial is possible, the doctor then goes on to foster even more denial.

Physical deterioration is not always matched by proportionate psychological changes. Fear of dying and of death may be more typical of early stages than of the latter phases of incurable illness. As time passes, people become more accepting of limitations, so that when death approaches, it is not always accompanied by growing fears. The absence of fear does not mean denial. If death were always an uncompromising adversary, then efforts to console each other would be merely self-serving platitudes.

The purpose of studying the dying process is to learn ways of helping people attain *significant survival*, so that as they near the end, they can also achieve a *purposeful death*. Sick people only become patients when they come under a doctor's care. The circumstances of "patienthood" often contribute more to a dying person's incapacity, suffering, and disorientation than does the specific disease itself. Cultural and social surroundings are seldom specified in the diagnosis and recording of illnesses. Yet, to omit these considerations means to ignore the capacity for viable behavior that the environment, human and inanimate, can generate. Sometimes, it is the influence of other people and the inherent dignity of their concern that make the difference between a meaningless and a purposeful death.

Significant survival is a quality of life that means much more than simply not to die. Purposeful death also means more than dying; it includes a measure of fulfillment, quiescence, resolution, and even traces of personal development. The notion of purposeful death can be misunderstood, however, and, therefore, I have included it in this section about misconceptions. Purposeful death can mislead, tempting the observer to impose his own wishes and constructions on the other person. As a result, it is easy to foster a misconception by endowing death with a mystical purpose and meaning that may only be in someone else's mind.

People die in different ways, some with full disposition and acceptance, but people do not die merely because death is acceptable. Nor do they die simply because they have the same disease. Regardless of anatomical diagnosis, physical deterioration, and clinical staging, there is no fixed formula of morbidity and mortality. Doctors deal with probabilities, not with absolutes, but while they know about probabilities, they must contend with individuals.

Our common misconception would confine sickness to the sickroom and disease to the patient. But sickness is always more comprehensive than the physical illness. People die to many things before they die, at last, from a disease. Seldom do we scrutinize the lethal factors and forces that delineate the field in which the substance of disease emerges.

In a later chapter, the topic of psychosocial death will be discussed more fully. Here, however, predilection and purposeful deaths elicit the psychological factors that are so dimly seen in most illnesses. Engel (1967, 1968) and Schmale (1964) have described how situations of giving up or being given up may precede instances of physical illness. Saul reported cases of death that happen at a critical impasse in a patient's life. When these documented cases are supplemented with deaths that occur under strange, nonorganic circumstances, we can, with modest justification, assume that unspecified emotional factors are significant determinants of the disposition to die.

In 1961, Weisman and Hackett reported a small series of patients who looked forward to death with yearning, acceptance, certainty, serenity, and even with a measure of impatience. Although these patients differed from each other, they shared the belief that death offered a promise of resolution and relief that further living did not. In effect, they had nothing more to live for, survival was distasteful and meaningless.

Because their patients seemed so willing to die, without the signs of denial and anxiety that most clinicians expect, Weisman and Hackett termed this "predilection to death." Since that time, other patients have faced death with quiet anticipation and without regret. Although some physicians have misunderstood their quiet resignation, calling it "depression" or "apathy," most predilected patients are not dejected.

Some patients are quite willing to die, but do not wish explicitly for death. Others want to die, but do not really expect to. Still more are sad and subdued, but are not convinced that death is at hand or on the threshold. Nevertheless, there are moments when the course of illness coincides with psychosocial transitions, and the result is death. Many patients, perhaps more than we imagine, heed the signs of impending death, and respond to the summons with a sense of purpose. They resist efforts to prolong life and accede to the thrust of extinction.

Although predilected deaths lack the drama of voodoo or psychogenic deaths, we can scarcely ignore the element of purpose and intentionality in such outcomes. Society prizes survival at almost any price. It is, therefore, difficult to imagine circumstances in which a combination of sickness and desire for death brings about a fatality. Nevertheless, organic processes and noxious events can potentiate each other, so it would be a misconception, should we disallow psychological and intentional deaths, short of suicide. If we then open up the possibility that some deaths may be predilected, and that some people contribute to their own extinction with a purpose, we shall contradict the age-old misconception that death is always and everywhere an evil, and never is an acceptable outcome. Furthermore, we will look for a purpose in death, because we would acknowledge that at least a few people can harmoniously die, with a minimum of denial and nullification.

APPROPRIATE AND APPROPRIATED DEATH

Every idea about death is a version of life. Concepts of heaven and hell, damnation and redemption, resolution of suffering, and rewards for deeds, good and ill, are simply extensions of what is already here. To look far into the future is largely an unrevealing pastime. Those events which we glimpse in the distant future are contemporary occasions, seen through the wrong end of a telescope. Even with thorough knowledge of someone's habits, thoughts, and style of life, we cannot accurately predict how and when he will come to the end of his life. Nor can we do this for ourselves. Like living, dying cannot be reduced to a small package of maxims. To tell another person what he ought to do, think, or be is an affront at any time; but to do this when he nears the end of life is sanctimonious cruelty.

We need not be very perceptive to realize that the unceasing destruction afflicting mankind supports the belief that death is senseless, unfair, painful, and tragic. Wars and calamities of nature somehow change our image of death, even giving it a bitter meaning. Where individual death is concerned, however, few of us would ever be prepared to die, if we did not die until we chose. Human beings struggle, suffer, falter, and ask for more. But when the margin between life and death blurs, as in many illnesses, people are then willing to slip quietly into oblivion. Indeed, were it possible for a few people in every generation to live on forever, we would soon cease thinking of them as members of the human race. This elite group might even be feared, like some monstrosity who could not die. Although in the flush of health, we may want to live on, and spontaneously assume that this is possible, the gift of immortality, were it available, might turn out to be a curse.

Appropriate death is a form of purposeful death, but not every instance of purposeful death is an appropriate death. To be willing to die does not mean that someone is able to die, or that his death would be appropriate. Death may be appropriate, but not acceptable; acceptable, but not appropriate. Obviously, appropriate death for one person might be unsuitable for another. Finally, what might seem appropriate from the outside, might be utterly meaningless to the dying person himself. Conversely, deaths that seem unacceptable to an outsider, might be desirable from the inner viewpoint of the patient.

Appropriated Death

Appropriate death has a superficial resemblance to rational suicide, i.e., self-elected death compatible with the ego ideal. In olden times, suicide was an option that ensured honor for certain steadfast people. Many famous men took their own life, instead of surrendering their principles or compromising integrity. A legendary contrast in two manners of suicide is that of Seneca who chose death by his own hand, as opposed to his pupil, Nero, who had to be forced into suicide.

Actually, suicides of great men are often misinterpreted as great and rational deeds, worthy of the man. But we may forget that a great man may be subject to deep depressions and fully capable of destroying himself without the exoneration of "good reasons." The school-book jingle that "Lives of great men all remind us/ We can make our lives sublime . . ." hides another fact, that the deaths of great men also show how mortal and fallible they can be. Who has the audacity to approve or disapprove of how anyone chooses to die, unless by his death, he nullifies whatever potential being alive holds? We can readily conjure up events that might justify self-destruction, but there are also circumstances in which murder could be condoned. An act of destruction might resolve conflict and relieve suffering, but for whom—the victim or the executioner?

It can be argued that to deprive man of his right to terminate life is an abridgement of his freedom. Yet, few suicides, rescued after an attempt, complain about their freedom, though they might regret being saved. The reasons that people assign to a suicide may be "good," but not the correct reasons. A man who is suicidal at 3 a.m. may find the idea unthinkable at 9 a.m., even though his reasons remain the same. One part of his personality decrees death for every other part. In a sense, suicide is an external agency that victimizes; the option to destroy oneself is not an expression of freedom, but one of despair. We lament a suicide; arguments for its freedom and rationality are only sophistries. Suffering of any origin is deplorable; any of us might choose to die before being completely tyrannized by disease or despotism. Few of us can predict with unerring certainty what we would do if . . . . Suicide must be construed as an emergency exit, not the main approach to a style of life. The suicide, for his own private reasons and intentionality, appropriates death for himself; he does not seek appropriate conditions in which to die. His death usually negates his ego ideal, and in other respects, as well, may be the antithesis of the conditions and circumstances for an appropriate death.

It is conceivable that at the very end of life, people can undergo changes in outlook, so that the meaning of having existed acquires a special significance. Appropriate death does not require complete knowledge about the dying person; few of us could satisfy these preconditions, even about ourselves! Appropriate death does require that we understand the contemporaneous experience that we call dying-in-the-here-and-now. The Greek word, Kairos, an auspicious moment that leads to a decisive change, can also be applied, to the event called dying. It is not an idealized image of death, nor does it delete the painful implications of dying to and from a number of things. The here-and-now significance of dying is very concrete, and should not be confused with the imaginary then-and-there of a "promised land." The dying person can, at best, only foresee a wisp of future time. Hence, the now-and-here has a pungency that draws upon every level and period of his existence. Like some memento, it is a unit of reality that may encompass a lifetime.

Conditions of an Appropriate Death

Someone who dies an appropriate death must be helped in the following ways: He should be relatively pain-free, his suffering reduced, and emotional and social impoverishments kept to a minimum. Within the limits of disability, he should operate on as high and effective a level as possible, even though only tokens of former fulfillments can be offered. He should also recognize and resolve residual conflicts, and satisfy whatever remaining wishes are consistent with his present plight and with his ego ideal. Finally, among his choices, he should be able to yield control to others in whom he has confidence. He also has the option of seeking or relinquishing significant key people.

Obviously, these conditions of an appropriate death are like the highest aspirations of mankind! Few people are ever fortunate enough to realize these goals. Consequently, it may seem most unlikely that people about to die could reach or even care about appropriate death, if the requirements are so unrealistic. On the other hand, our preconception that death can *never* be appropriate may be a self-fulfilling idea. If we believe that death is bad, and dying people, by a magical contagion, are tainted, then appropriate deaths are never possible. By discouraging therapeutic intercessions, therefore, we may contribute deep alienation, hopelessness, and loneliness.

Given a measure of consciousness, control, and competence to work with, we can encourage appropriate death, or at least a purposeful death. Patients can, for example, be protected from needless procedures that only dehumanize and demean, without offering suitable compensation. We can, moreover, ask people how much consciousness is desirable. Some patients prefer solitude toward the end in order to collect their thoughts. Others, more gregarious, need family and friends. As life ebbs away, some patients want to doze, while others prefer to be alert, and to simulate the regular periods of sleep and wakefulness that healthy people enjoy.

If we refuse to think of appropriate death as a quixotic vision beyond reach, we will protect the patient's autonomy and personal dignity. Much, of course, depends upon the concern of the key participants. Although most people tremble at the notion of dying, it is wholly practical that they can offer a substantial contribution to the mutual task. An appropriate death, in brief, is a death that someone might choose for himself—had he a choice. The central idea, of course, is that to foster an appropriate death, one must realize that death is not an ironic choice without an option, but a way of living as long as possible. Our task is therefore to separate death and its prejudices from each other.

4

Case Material and Methods

Thousands of people die of fatal illnesses each year, but even in large medical centers and teaching hospitals, few psychiatrists actively participate in the diagnosis and treatment of these patients. Despite extensive efforts and elaborate programs to introduce principles of psychological medicine into patient care, psychosocial elements of illness are rarely heeded and seldom reported on the case records. Physical findings, laboratory data, and medical histories are meticulously documented, but there is little information about the patient's life style, personality, and sociopsychological circumstances. When included at all in the day-by-day operation and practice of medicine, psychological information is relegated to the rear, as if segregation underscored its second-class status.

As a rule, even general hospital psychiatrists tend to deal only with patients who are not very sick. Psychiatric education is also scaled in such a way that the more senior and experienced a psychiatrist becomes, the less contact he has with patients on medical and surgical wards. He finds himself in a supervisory or teaching role that minimizes direct participation in case management. As a result, the combination of junior psychiatrists and a medical tradition that tacitly excludes emotional and social factors creates a situation in which psychiatrists have little experience and, therefore, little to offer in the management of critically ill patients.

Our project, the study of death and denial, was bound to meet problems of referral and case selection. In addition to the ambivalent version of what psychiatry does, does not, and cannot do, physicians are understandably reluctant to refer seriously ill patients. Many doctors share the misconception that psychiatric interviews can make a patient worse than many diagnostic and surgical procedures which are undertaken without hesitation. There is a permissiveness about recommending almost any kind of physical intervention, even if it produces more distress than benefit. The social sanction about "doing everything possible" for a dying patient does not, unfortunately, extend to psychiatric assessment. Actually, some physicians consider that a psychiatric consultation would be an affront to a patient with a fatal illness.

In finding suitable case material for study, we were aware that colleagues are like people everywhere: They had mixed feelings, doubt, and dogmatism about death and dying. They approved of the general study, but disapproved of interviewing dying patients. In effect, they were cooperative and uncooperative, fair-minded and biased, sympathetic and antagonistic.

Despite the inherent difficulties, we conducted interviews with over 350 patients during the period of the investigation, 1962-1965. They were referred from various sources and in different stages of illness. In general, the bulk of our case material consisted of (a) cancer patients, (b) aged people suffering from different illnesses and degrees of senescence,

(c) myocardial infarction patients, many of whom were on the Danger List when first interviewed, (d) pre- and post-operative patients who were thought to be potentially terminal by the staff, the patient, or both, and (e) psychiatric patients who were conspicuously preoccupied with death. Many patients were found in the course of psychiatric consultations to medical and surgical services. Others were private referrals, and a few patients came to our attention simply by chance. In the latter part of the study, Cushing Hospital, a state-supported facility for the care of the aged, provided an opportunity through Dr. Robert Kastenbaum to evaluate at first hand, how the very aged face the closing-off of life. We excluded children, adolescents, depressed patients who were in no danger of dying, patients who were admitted because of a suicide attempt, people who were bereaved but not threatened with their own death, and terminal patients who were too moribund, too heavily sedated, or too inarticulate to cooperate in an interview.

METHOD OF STUDY

We relied exclusively on the interview method. Every patient was interviewed by one or both of the psychiatrists, and many were also seen by Mrs. Ruth Abrams and Mrs. Margaret Heywood, social workers who were affiliated with the project at different times.

In addition to speaking frequently with the patients, there were consultations with the professional staff and conversations with families and friends of patients. The number of interviews ranged from a single contact to long-term relationships that sometimes continued long after the patient's death, and included members of the patient's family.

It was appropriate to begin with the special method of interviewing, assessment, and interaction that we had developed over a number of years for use on medical and surgical wards (Hackett & Weisman, 1960). This method, called *the psychotherapeutic consultation*, grew out of a need to give practical application to the concept of the patient as a unique and responsible individual, instead of as just the passive bearer of disease. As our experience in dealing with the dying developed, we modified the format of the psychotherapeutic consultation in accordance with the special problems that psychosocial intervention elicited (Weisman & Hackett, 1962).

The primary diagnosis is not a reliable clue for assessing personal responses and individual reactions. Variations in behavior differ greatly from the signs and symptoms of disease; many are responses to personal crises and conflicts, and eluded efforts to describe them in conventional terms.

Psychotherapeutic Consultation

The earlier format of the psychotherapeutic consultation gradually changed and became the *participatory interview*, as we attempted to elicit the personal dimensions of illness. The method is intended to allow the investigator to go beyond the confines of *disease-orientation* to a more comprehensive view of illness, based upon *person-orientation*.

Person-orientation is based upon a theory of context, not of causation. The concept of "cause" is an inappropriate concept in behavioral studies and psychosomatic medicine. At best, "cause" is an abstraction drawn from the larger field of forces in which sickness develops.

In its actual application, the participatory interview has two major aspects, called the *extended evaluation* and the *encounter*. Both require the active participation of the psychiatrist himself, not merely as a detached observer, but as an effective agent himself (Weisman, 1961). The extended evaluation directs the psychiatrist to formulate salient problems as succinctly as possible, and then to implement his recommendations during continued patient care. The encounter is the way that doctor and patient come together at a moment of high vulnerability. The purpose is not merely to evaluate, but to exchange information and to modify and correct their mutual behavior. The person facing death is, of course, in a precarious plight. But, to some extent, every psychiatrist who finds himself in this situation, encounters his own mortality in ways that most physicians are able to avoid. He recognizes that the problems of death and dying are not wholly determined by disease, but are critical transitions in a person's relationship with his familiar world. His continuing contact assures the patient of his availability. If he is clear about his own misgivings and apprehensions, the psychiatrist will then be able to be open and accessible.

The strategy of the participatory interview is that the psychiatrist should match his approach with the appropriate dimension of the patient's illness that is being investigated. For example, when seeking objective or impersonal information, such as the reasons for referral, the facts of illness, recent treatment, predominant symptoms, and so forth, the psychiatrist adopts an impersonal approach. When asking about interpersonal or transactional factors, such as job history, family relations, illnesses and deaths among friends and family in the recent past, financial and social status, and so forth, the investigator follows a much more humane and interpersonal approach. The most delicate dimension to assess is the patient's intrapersonal response to his life-and-death condition. The doctor will not hesitate to make use of his own enlightened subjectivity. He will find that spontaneity and acceptance often enable him to see beneath verbal camouflage. Although he may misunderstand a great deal, a frankly personal attitude in which the doctor emerges as a person himself encourages the patient to be more candid. In contrast to adopting a forced objectivity, interview material will be much more spontaneous, although somewhat more unsystematic.

Point of Maximum Interest

Patients differed greatly in their ability to communicate, as well as in their diagnosis, stage of illness, disability, denial, and medical symptoms. Naturally, we came to know those patients best whom we could evaluate over a period of time and with reasonable confidence. It may be true that every patient shows something of interest or illustrates in his own way the workings of a larger principle. But it is equally true that some patients demonstrate the same problem more clearly than others.

Twenty-five patients were seen at least 12 times or were followed for several months. Because we knew them best, they were called "in-depth" patients. Fifty patients who were interviewed less than 12 times were also so articulate that we could study some distinct issue or problem related to death and denial. These brief but revealing contacts were called "vignettes." In other words, there were 75 patients with whom we had sufficiently prolonged or intensive relationships to warrant confident judgments about their attitudes and experiences in the presence of death.

Fifty additional patients illustrated various clinical and theoretical problems, but could not be followed carefully or long enough to qualify as "in-depth" or "vignette" patients. We used this clinical material to supplement information drawn from better known patients. The remainder of the patients, at least 200 more, when we counted various consultations, were appraised by searching the material for any additional clinical finding, problem, symptom, and issue that might yield insight into the dying process. We found, however, that these patients showed nothing so startling or revealing that better-known patients had not already demonstrated. It was not possible to draw statistical conclusions about such a scattered group. Factors that made some patients "better-known" than others could not be standardized. Our principal aim, therefore, was to find points of maximum interest in every patient that would disclose how the encounter with death takes place. This meant, of course, that there were undoubtedly points of maximum interest that illness, debility, derangements, limitations of time, and our own lack of perceptiveness prevented us from finding. No one can be completely understood by another person, and there were many observations that could not be related to whatever else we knew. Better-known patients usually showed many points of maximum interest, simply because they were observed over a longer time. This finding, however obvious, points up the limitations of studies that are based upon only one or two interviews. The better one knows a patient, or anyone else, for that matter, the less stereotyped his personality becomes. His responses are more fluid, and his signs of health and strength shine through the curtain of illness. Under hospital circumstances, the psychology of death can only be partially fathomed. In the unfolding drama of death, dying, denying, and decline, the script and scenes shift according to the exigencies of the moment and are shaped by the format that disease imposes. The following case illustrates how points of maximum interest may be limited by the hospital perspective, but when the patient is followed for a long time, it becomes clear that sickness is far too important to be left for physicians.

Case 1. Eight months before he was admitted to the hospital, a 38-year-old equipment salesman developed pains and weakness in both legs. Because these symptoms started while he was sitting on a hard bench for several hours, waiting for his wife to give birth to their first child, local doctors assumed that his complaints were "psychosomatic." For the next six months, he was treated with analgesics and physical therapy. Two months before admission, however, X-ray disclosed widespread metastases to the cervical and lumbar vertebrae. Further study then revealed carcinoma of the kidney.

FIRST HOSPITAL ADMISSION
Both the patient and his wife knew the diagnosis and the pessimistic outlook. His legs had become so weak and the pains so severe that it was no longer possible to remain at home. He was not only aware of his condition, but realized that even his search for relief might be futile.

He readily accepted the suggestion of a psychiatric consultation and was not at all reluctant to talk about his personal plight. As a result, his forthright manner quickly endeared him to the psychiatrist, just as he had won the interest and respect of the surgical staff. Largely, this attitude and response resulted from his belief, simple and unassuming, that everyone would help as much as possible, to the limits of their skill. Consequently, he did not plead, did not seek false reassurance, and at no time expressed self-pity.

SOCIAL HISTORY
The patient grew up on a farm in northern New England, the third son of four children. He married early, and earned his living as a logger, sheet metal worker, and, more recently, as an equipment salesman. However, from time to time, when the routine of daily life began to pall, he would leave his job and family to set out for the wilderness for a few days. There, without extensive equipment or supplies, he would live off the land, sleep in the open, find his food by fishing and trapping, until he regained a sense of self-reliance and autonomy.

His first marriage was unsatisfactory from the start. After ten years, his wife joined a fundamentalist religious sect, and the marriage deteriorated still further. She argued frequently, disregarded the household, ceased bathing, required sexual abstinence, and went to nightly prayer meetings.

Several years before divorcing his first wife, he met a married woman who worked as a waitress to support her two children and indigent husband. He then spent the next few years trying to save enough money from his meager income to buy a second-hand motorcycle and pay for a trip to Nevada and a divorce. Once again, he tested his self-reliance and capacity to survive under difficult conditions. His staunchly conservative family opposed his decision, when he made it known, and he was ostracized by neighbors and friends. Some of these people never forgave him, even when he was dying.

Two years before being stricken with cancer, he was able to be married at last. Nevertheless, in looking back, he declared that if he had not had two years of happy marriage, his life would have been a complete waste. He recalled how his first wife cursed him, predicting that he would never live to enjoy a second marriage. Furthermore, his wife's first husband had excused his indigency by claiming to have an incurable illness that doctors could not diagnose. Later, the patient's wife ruefully observed her first husband, still walking around their home town in a state of constant ill-health, while her present husband, who was proud of his ruggedness, independence, and productive labor, was doomed to die. Nevertheless, many of their fellow-townspeople felt that his fatal illness was appropriate punishment for wayward behavior.

INTERIM EVENTS AND OTHER HOSPITALIZATIONS

The patient had two later hospitalizations, both of which were for relief of pain. He had extensive neurosurgical treatment, with only transitory relief. His other problem was to support his family. He knew that his small insurance policy would not last long, and that his wife would have to work again.

Between bouts of pain, his morale was excellent. He compared his own plight with that of an older brother who had a tumor removed from his groin five years before. Although his brother returned to work, with no sign of recurrence, the patient still deplored the tension in his brother's household. Despite the difference in outcome, the patient preferred the way in which he and his wife faced the future with candor and love.

His physical problems became worse after discharge, and his financial worries were relieved no more effectively. He was paraplegic in his legs, as well as afflicted with constant pain in the left shoulder and arm. Lesions in the high cervical vertebrae made it impossible to perform a cordotomy. The family was officially on welfare, but according to the wife, the punitive attitude of the community led to unnecessary delays in getting enough food and drugs for relief of pain. The local physician challenged the use of narcotics, insisting that he had to send for morphine and dilaudid. Even then, the patient or his wife had to beg for the few pills he ordered. As a result, intervals between medication became longer and longer, and his pain became more uncontrollable. His former self-reliance could scarcely be preserved under these conditions. Now, he thought of himself only as a "charity case", who could not act on his own behalf. Fortunately, he found a temporary benefactor in a retired executive and his wife, a former nurse, who allowed the family to live rent-free in a gardener's cottage on their farm.

When he was next admitted to the hospital for further efforts to relieve pain, the patient had become thoroughly demoralized by pain and poverty. His rugged openness had gone, as had the nurses and doctors he had known before. His cooperation changed to captious criticism of hospital procedures, and as a result, the new staff failed to give him appropriate support. Actually, he was not treated badly, but rather as just another terminal patient for whom little could be done. Perhaps for this reason, he was transferred, without explanation, to another ward where he was totally unknown. The procedures in the new ward were wholly unfamiliar. Despite his debilitated state, he was expected to conform without complaint. Inadvertently, he interpreted the impersonal treatment received in the hospital as rebuff and neglect, an attitude that had been forced upon him by his punitive home town. He became openly irate and accusatory, and this caused the staff to exhibit even more indifference and started a regrettable "positive feedback" situation.

As his relationships deteriorated, denial increased. Neither parent had visited him, but he found reasons to justify their neglect. On one occasion, he exclaimed, "I know that if I really needed them, they'd be here!" He did not mention the circumstances in which he would be in greater need than the present.

His relationship with the psychiatrist also became more remote. Because of the family's financial and emotional problems, the psychiatrist telephoned the patient's sister, hoping that she would be less punitive and more helpful. Several days later, she did visit, and after a tearful reunion, promised to take care of her brother's needs. However, the promise was not kept, nor did the patient hear from her again.

For a short time, following his sister's visit, the patient's morale improved. Then he relapsed after an altercation with an interne who rebuked him for smoking, saying that he would not need so much medication if he did not smoke. The patient was indignant, yet felt powerless; once again, he was being punished, because he knew that the interne had spoken out of puritanical prejudice, not medical information.

His physical status was not more satisfactory than his morale. Nerve blocks were ineffective, and the shoulder pain was unrelenting. He had a dream in which he and his father were trying to break up a log jam in the river back home. After much effort and conspicuous cooperation between the man and boy, the logs slowly began to give way . . . then he awakened with a resurgence of pain down his arm.

On his good days, he hoped that somehow he could beat the death sentence. On bad days, he was surly, confused, somnolent. Sometimes he believed that he heard jackhammers outside his window, implying that he could no longer distinguish pain and noise. Later, unexpected interruptions, a knock, sounds of voices all fused into a constant barrage of suffering. Then he fell and sustained a pathological fracture of the femur. For the first time, his denial became so prominent that he seemingly forgot about his diagnosis. He assumed that his main difficulty was the fracture, and that he would be well in about 6 months. This statement was based upon the orthopedist's judgment that fractures of the femur usually require about 6 months of treatment before patients can walk again. There was no mention of the cancer and the imminence of death. A few days later, he asked the psychiatrist when he would be able to drive his car again! The patient seemed surprised when the doctor wondered where he wanted to go, and answered, "Why, I just want to ride up and down the coast visiting my relatives. Maybe I'll drive down to see my sister."

His many complaints about "poor care" were readily understood as referring to his steady deterioration, as if poor care meant poor progress. At this time the psychiatrist, also, began to withdraw. He visited the patient less often and found trivial excuses for staying away. The patient's denial was more pronounced. For example, one day he asked why the medicine wasn't helping, adding the comment that "It isn't as if I were dying or something!" When pressed on this point, he mumbled something about not feeling sick, in contradiction to his complaints of a moment before. After being reminded that he would not be in the hospital, were he not sick, the patient replied that while he didn't feel very good, "sick" meant to be nauseated, and he was at least not bothered by that!

Shortly afterward, he was discharged from the hospital on his own request. The staff believed that he had reached a point of maximum hospital benefit. It was not unreasonable to send him home, from the staff's viewpoint, even without adequate provisions for care. Nothing more was available, unless it was the death that seemed closer than ever. Despite acceptance of the inevitable, the psychiatrist still found himself resenting the patient and his wife. The reasons for this rather unreasonable response were obscure, until the doctor realized that by keeping the patient in the hospital, he could cling to the vain hope that death might be postponed.

TERMINAL PERIOD

The psychiatrist had visited the patient almost every week, after the patient's first hospitalization. Now, after his recent discharge, the trip became burdensome and fruitless. Instead, the patient's wife was encouraged to write reports periodically about her husband's condition. This maneuver was intended to help her gain some understanding about delirium and confusion, but it also gave her something more personal to do than housekeeping and basic nursing care.

He seldom spoke of death during the terminal period. When the 6-month recovery period for the femoral fracture ended, without tangible improvement in walking, he said nothing. He seemed unconcerned about fresh metastases to the chest wall, and spoke as if they were "muscle ruptures." The community's hostility changed into indifference; financial problems continued. His wife now looked for further signs of neglect and insult. Then, as time began to run out, a few old friends reappeared. Even his estranged son, now 21 years old, called upon him, and they became reconciled. His wife wrote, "He gets so much comfort from just knowing that people care."

One night, he told her not to change the bedsheets because he was going home. She thought he was telling her about death, but it is also possible that he had somehow confused the procedure with that in the hospital. Pain diminished, and his drug requirements lessened. His senses dulled, but his olfaction became hyperacute. A casual acquaintance called one evening and read the Lord's Prayer aloud. Thereafter, to his wife's surprise, this became a nightly routine, although he had not been a religious man and had reason to resent the intrusion of fundamentalist doctrines and abstemious practices into his first marriage. On one of his infrequent visits, the psychiatrist found that although the patient knew life was vanishing, he still expected to become an old man!

Four weeks before death, he developed an acute urinary infection.

He demanded that he be permitted to walk, and then became extremely alarmed when he realized that neither walking nor urination was possible.

Despite his growing confusion and delirium, he showed a disarmingly accurate recollection for events of his boyhood. But then he gradually became incoherent; conversation was impossible. One week before he died, his narcotic requirements almost ceased entirely, possibly because the cancer had at last produced the cordotomy that neurosurgery had been unable to provide. Two days before death, his wife wrote that he seemed to look better, to complain less, and to be more alert and talkative than he had been in weeks. "If I didn't know exactly where we stood, I would think that he was getting better!"

This long but still sketchy record reveals many points of maximum interest, ranging from the brief episode of premortem clarity and false improvement to the far more critical problems of secondary suffering induced by poverty and community punishment. Despite his healthy acceptance of the tragic interruption to his life and marriage, circumstances prevented an appropriate or dignified death. Loyalty and devotion could not compensate for impoverishment and alienation from his family and friends. It was also significant that his lesion could not be relieved by surgical means. Thus, he was wholly dependent upon fluctuation in surrounding events. Whenever a disheartening setback occurred, as with the pathological fracture, his denial became more pronounced.

Perhaps the most significant issue is that the kind of death he underwent, together with the extensive secondary suffering, was largely determined by nonmedical factors. Pain and paralysis might not have been relieved by more money or more community respect, but it is plausible that alienation and abandonment aggravated his terminal deterioration, just as in the hospital, episodes in which he felt misunderstood, ignored, or cared for poorly seemed to mirror changes in his physical condition.

We must also point out that, long after self-reliance had vanished and he had become someone who could scarcely bargain for relief, he responded with almost miraculous warmth to the reconciliation with his son and brother. He even returned to a boyhood affiliation with religion, suggesting that for him, the Lord's Prayer and community acceptance belonged together. Hence, his death illustrated many factors that exacerbate and relieve the anguish of dying. His lesion was not accessible to surgical relief, and he was helped only fleetingly by narcotics. But, had he unlimited access to adequate medication and nursing care, had his family and community supported him instead of punishing him, it is reasonable to assume that hopelessness and secondary suffering would have been substantially alleviated.

5

Denial and Middle Knowledge

SURVIVAL AND FATAL ILLNESS

For most people, sickness is uncomfortable, inconvenient, temporary, but rarely a menace. Then, if sickness persists, enduring beyond the healing effects of treatment and time, the personal dimensions of being sick gradually become more conspicuous. Prolonged illness means not only primary derangements in bodily functions and organs, but secondary incapacity of otherwise intact organs and functions. Like the sick person himself, physical functions and organs may be affected by having nothing to do. Healthy activity requires that we have tasks to perform. If this is not possible, everyday performance becomes more and more difficult until we deteriorate into someone who is concerned merely about the meager necessities of survival alone.

Health means far more than simply not being sick. Similarly, recovery from an illness means more than merely being able to survive. There is a dimension of health that assures us of gratification in being able to do for ourselves. We are not only able to survive, but can act on our own behalf according to the values and standards of the ego ideal.

The patient who is afflicted with a potentially fatal illness is forced to contend with both a threatening disease and impairment of his personal significance. The healing effect of treatment and time are not his. Therefore, as his illness progresses, he is forced to settle for less and less, to compromise his expectations, and to become less than what he had been or might be. Finally, survival becomes an end in itself. He is cut off from most of the satisfactions and significance that he had enjoyed and in which he had found most of his personal meaning.

The process of dying takes place in many ways and on different levels of experience. We die to many things before we die of a disease. Small, partial deaths gradually become confluent, so that we may cease to be as an autonomous person long before literal terminus takes place.

The full sense of viability is determined by three factors: (a) biological survival, (b) competent behavior, and (c) responsible conduct.

Biological survival in the course of serious illness means physical continuity, pain relief, reduction of suffering, and adaptation to diminished strength and capacity. *Competent behavior* means that, to some extent, a sick person can choose the way in which he solves daily problems and carries out his customary tasks. *Responsible conduct* is determined by how closely a patient's competence permits him to fulfill the directives and avoid the prohibitions dictated by his ego ideal.

These three factors contribute to the complete meaning of viability, which is *significant survival*, not merely biological existence. Organic disease can precipitate sickness, but not all sickness is due to disease. Many nonorganic factors and processes enter into survival and recovery, and can aggravate, precipitate, and redirect the course of illness. Moreover, sickness and its resolution may require a strategy of adaptation to the various psychosocial issues generated by organic incapacity. To a significant degree, assessment of denial is based upon the extent and style in which a patient accepts and repudiates the personal impact of sickness.

THE MECHANISM CALLED DENIAL

Few books in the literature of psychiatry have been as influential as Anna Freud's *The ego and the mechanisms of defence* (1948). Stripped to essentials, its major contribution is a theory that defense mechanisms are based upon a primitive response to danger called *denial*. Although A. Freud confined her examples to children, describing denial by word, act, and fantasy, her viewpoint could readily be expanded to include more differentiated and sophisticated defenses, as found in adults. Indeed, a wholly appropriate title might have been, "The ego and the mechanisms of denial."

Since her book, many psychiatrists have described more elaborate forms of defenses and have extended the concept of denial. As a result, "denial" now covers almost any situation, act, or verbal expression in which anyone seeks to "avoid reality," or to escape confrontation with something unpleasant and alarming, at least in the opinion of the observer.

Lewin (1950) asserted that denial is necessary for mood-enhancing and manic states. He compared the manic patient to an infant who has been stimulated and satisfied in a feeding relationship with mother. Eating, sucking, sleeping, and dreamless death are not only closely allied in Lewin's opinion, but can be induced by extensive denial.

Fenichel's encyclopedic treatise on psychoneurosis (1945) depends upon the idea that denial permeates practically the entire range of psychopathology. Schizophrenic reactions, fetishism, memory defects, anxiety attacks, sleep disturbances, and even seizures are attributed to the excessive operation of the mechanism called denial. His hypothesis seems to be that denial is always available whenever a person is threatened, from whatever source. Its usual effect is to negate a painful perception or to neutralize a distressing conflict. By frequent reiteration, the reader gains the impression that denial is a mechanism that can be set in motion by any crisis or conflict, and that most defenses, if not all symptoms, depend upon denial.

In general, denial has been used as a fictitious *mechanism*, an *as if* entity that can be triggered promptly by a threatening event or perception, as well as a hypothetical *explanation* for different kinds of psychopathology. Anna Freud regarded denial as a *unifying* concept for different defenses, but she did not suggest that denial is a *unitary* mechanism which serves only to repudiate reality. In fact, she pointed out that denial is expressed in words, acts, and fantasies, but these are what people *do* in order to counter, neutralize, and reorient themselves in the presence of danger. In other words, denial is but one aspect of what defenses do. Denial helps us to do away with a threatening portion of reality, but only because we may then participate more fully in contending with problems.

Terminology simplifies communication, but it can often defeat itself. Terms such as "denial" and "defense mechanisms" are outstanding examples of "misplaced concreteness." Not only are these terms frequently assumed to represent well-established entities, but they are used as explanatory concepts. When this happens, further inquiry and investigation are tacitly discouraged, because custom decides that the words are synonymous with the facts. For example, were we to assume that "memory" is synonymous with "remembering," and that it was a basic, irreducible mental fact, then we would not be able to analyze remembering further. We would be oblivious to the complexities of how information is acquired, registered, stored, scanned, and retrieved.

Psychiatrists often speak about defense mechanisms as if they were independent mental operations which are almost dissociated from the ebb and flow of interpersonal events. They imply that defenses are characteristic of each individual, and that external "dangers" simply elicit a familiar response, with comparatively little selectivity. Defenses are very real events, but the hypothesis designating the reality of defense mechanisms is very dubious. Defenses are ways in which the individual selectively participates in on-going events, but defense "mechanisms" are only general terms which characterize broad similarities between them. There is nothing fundamentally wrong about generalizing acts and statements that separate us from a threatening situation, and calling the effect "denial," unless we believe that denial is the exclusive function of an inner mechanism whose sole purpose is to mitigate the meaning of an external danger.

We must distinguish between the *process of denying* and the *fact of denial*. Denial is a total process of responding within a specific psychosocial context. Negation is only one of the consequences of this process; denial is a final fact, not the process itself. To confuse a total process with one of its defensive aims is like saying that the purpose of driving an automobile is to avoid accidents.

THE PROCESS CALLED DENYING

The mechanistic interpretation of denial has wholly a negative aim—to avoid a painful perception, or, more generally, to keep a distance between a perception and the person who is frightened by it. However, any purposeful act may have its defensive side which serves the aim of avoidance and aversion. The familiar expression, "using denial," suggests that denial is a primary defense, having no other function but that of aversion and negation. In contrast with this mechanistic interpretation, the dynamic interpretation of denial does not accept negation and aversion as static products of a process, but rather as incomplete interpretations of a variety of related acts.

The process called denying is both an act and a fact—the act of denying and the fact of denial. Both depend upon personal interaction to define what, how, and when denying takes place.

The act of denying precedes the fact of denial by four successive steps. These steps are:

1. Acceptance of a primary and public field of perception.
2. Repudiation of a portion of the shared meaning of that field.
3. Replacement of the repudiated meaning with a more congenial version.
4. Reorientation of the individual within the scope of the total meaning, in order to accommodate the revised reality.

The fifth step brings about the fact of denial.

Acceptance of a primary and public field of perception means that no one can deny by himself, in utter solitude. He may repudiate events or flee from an impending danger, but he cannot deny unless a portion of that field is shared with someone else.

Repudiation of a portion of the shared meaning may take place by simple negation, but a person may also behave inappropriately for the existing situation, as if the painful portion of the field were not perceived or shared with anyone else. Directly or indirectly, *replacement* of the repudiated meaning occurs. *Reorientation* means that not only is the threat contained or, possibly, excluded from the field, but earlier relationships and prior conditions are restored.

From the inside, people do not recognize that they have denied a reality, whether it is a perception or a meaning. They only know that every action, aggressive and aversive, is affirmative, fight, flight, or immobilization. The only criterion for understanding its meaning is whether the act is effective and accurate. Only in retrospect do people sometimes see that they have avoided, denied, or negated an obvious reality. The *fact* of denial needs another person who judges that denial of their shared reality has occurred. But the fact of denial means more than simply the presence of an outside judge. Shared and public realities are as much created as contended with. We test reality, but part of the process called "reality testing" is that we are tested by reality, as well. In the interpersonal field, we test out our perceptions and performances, but we are also tested by others seeking confirmation of their realities. Consequently, whenever anyone alters the meaning of a commonly accepted reality, declaring that his version is correct, he can expect to be challenged, simply because everyone within a specific field needs to protect and reaffirm what seems self-evident to him.

The mechanistic interpretation of denial is static, because it does not allow for the modulating participation of the other person to whom the denial is expressed. It assumes that denial is a constant, and that someone who denies does so out of his inner workings, not in order to redefine a relationship with another person in a specific context. As a rule, clinicians tend to ignore the significance of the external observer or participant in making the diagnosis of denial.

They assume that denial is merely a matter of more-or-less deviation from an accepted norm, which usually means their own. Depending upon whether a patient is thought to deny a great deal or hardly at all, some doctors recognize major, partial, and minor denial. Patients who minimize are thought to show minor denial, while those who substitute delusions for reality are major deniers.

As a rule, denial is found most frequently when the doctor looks for it, least often when he takes his patient's statements at face value. Naturally, any judge presumes his own accuracy. But sometimes, inappropriate answers to questions may be the correct response, providing that the judge can correct for his special viewpoint and bias. Expectations often determine responses, and this is equally true when judging the extent of denial.

THE PURPOSE OF DENIAL

It is not enough merely to decide that someone has denied a self-evident reality. What form does the denial take? To whom is the denial communicated? What are the circumstances in which denial is expressed? What is threatened?

Although a potential danger is apt to evoke denial (as I shall call the combined act and fact), a common threatened danger is a *jeopardized relationship with a significant key person.* Hence, the purpose of denial is not simply to avoid a danger, but to prevent loss of a significant relationship (Weisman & Hackett, 1967). This explains why patients tend to deny more to certain people than to others. Patients who deny a great deal seem to do so in order to preserve a high level of self-esteem. For this reason, they need to preserve contact and stabilize their relationship with someone essential to self-esteem. Even when there seems to be no one in particular who threatens or could be threatened by a patient's illness, deterioration, or death, the patient himself may deny because he wants to maintain the *status quo* of already existing relationships.

> *Case 2.* A 48-year-old married woman with advanced, but not terminal cancer of the cervix was admitted to the hospital for further evaluation and treatment. She seemed calm, even optimistic, and behaved as if hospitalization would be only perfunctory. A social worker, who had known her for a long time, found it strange that this intelligent woman asked no questions about her own condition. She seemed much more preoccupied with her husband's duodenal ulcer than with her cancer. Despite many previous discussions, the patient seemed to ignore the uncertainty of the treatment, with the ultimate uncertainty about life itself.
>
> The extent of denial was so baffling that a psychiatric consultant was called upon. Almost as soon as the interview began, the patient suddenly asked, "Tell me, Doctor, is Grade 3 carcinoma of the cervix more malignant than Grade 1?" She then went on to talk about her serious condition, with no evidence of further denial. Her concern about the husband's ulcer stemmed from worry about how he would get along after her death. She had phrased her worry in terms of his proper diet, but the significant concern was whether he could keep the family together. There had been many arguments between her husband and their children. Without her intercession, she feared that the children would leave home, and, as a result, her husband's ulcer might get worse.

What prompted this patient to talk about her death with the consultant? She had already discussed these concerns with her social worker, but in the hospital, she denied worry, except to the psychiatrist, someone she had not seen before and, probably, would not see again. We should also note that she used an ostensibly medical question as a means of introducing more important problems.

This apparent paradox is very common: patients with serious illnesses will ask about their diagnosis and prognosis, but only to someone not in authority, such as a ward aide, a medical student, a consultant. These are, in effect, not significant people, so the patient can venture to speak with them about deeper concerns, not risking a rupture of significant relationships.

Denial helps to maintain a simplified, yet constant relationship with significant others, especially at a moment of crisis. Case 2 feared that she might lose her family as a result of her illness, part of which was symbolized by hospital admission. If she could manage to reduce the threat through denial, claiming that hospitalization was brief and trivial, that her husband's ulcer was more important, then already existing relationships could be preserved.

MIDDLE KNOWLEDGE

Somewhere between open acknowledgment of death and its utter repudiation is an area of uncertain certainty called *middle knowledge*. Case 1, for example, accepted death as an abstract plausibility. However, at moments of stress, such as after the pathological fracture, or shortly before his death, he voiced plans for a healthy future, or at least spoke about doing things that terminal illness precluded.

As a rule, middle knowledge tends to occur at serious transition points, such as when a patient begins the descent to death, undergoes a setback, or finds obvious equivocation among the people on whom he depends. Fluctuation between denial and acceptance takes place throughout the course of illness, except that denial is more readily diagnosed when there is less reason to hope.

Case 3. A 35-year-old widow entered the hospital for diagnostic evaluation. She had had a mastectomy several years earlier, but until recently, no further symptoms developed. Shortly after the tests were completed, it became apparent that despite slight clinical symptoms, she had extensive metastases. The problem of planning further treatment for what seemed to be a hopeless situation led to equivocation among her doctors, protracted bedside discussions, and unexplained delay in discharge. Although the doctors had been quite candid before, now they talked in riddles, each one contradicting the other. She asked to go home, but then, for no good reason, she was asked to stay a while longer.

In a conversation with the psychiatric consultant, the patient seemed to recognize the full import of her diagnosis, but then talked as if she had many years left and could even go back to work. She could not grasp the current treatment difficulties and was puzzled by her symptoms. Her operation had been so long ago, she complained, why was she so very weak now? A few days later, she lapsed into stupor, and died.

Middle knowledge is marked by unpredictable shifts in the margin between what is observed and what is inferred. Patients seem to know and want to know, yet they often talk as if they did not know and did not want to be reminded of what they have been told. Many patients rebuke their doctors for not having warned them about complications in treatment or the course of illness, even though the doctors may have been scrupulous about keeping them informed. These instances of seeming denial are usually examples of middle knowledge that herald a relapse. When a patient with a fatal illness suddenly becomes unable to draw plausible inferences about himself, slipping back into an exacerbation of denial, it is often a sign that the terminal phase is about to begin.

DEGREES OF DENIAL

Any statement can be contradicted, and our mental apparatus can nullify any reality, including its own. The roots of denial are planted in the biological, social, and emotional soil of life, not in the rules of logic. The various interactions that give rise to denial are so fluid and diversified that it is quite impossible to catalogue all the forms in which denial expresses itself. Even when we restrict the manifestations of denying and denial to the topic of threatened and incipient death, the scope of denial is never exhausted. People may deny facts about illness, symptoms, diagnosis, causes of illness, treatment, outlook, disability, family history, relationships, social resources, and, of course, impending death.

The familiar triad established by A. Freud does not mean that denial by word, act, or fantasy adequately classifies all forms of denying and denial. Words, acts, and fantasies are general ways in which we get to know another person. What he says, does, or thinks about are clues to his personality, whether he denies or not. Denying is a process, not a static event, so degrees of denial are never constant. Someone who is a major denier at one moment and under certain circumstances may be a minor denier in another situation.

Because this study was primarily concerned with denial as it related to terminality and the threat of death, our classification was based upon three degrees or orders of denial pertaining to death. *First-order denial* is based upon how a patient perceives the primary facts of illness. *Second-order denial* refers to the inferences that a patient draws, or fails to draw, about the extensions and implications of his illness. *Third-order denial* is concerned with the image of death itself: denial of extinction.

Denial of Facts

First-order denial is usually unequivocal from the observer's viewpoint. Because the discrepancy between a patient's report and perceptions and what the observer sees is so great, he has little difficulty in deciding that denial is present. For example, one aged woman refused to accept the fact of her son's death from cancer. Despite efforts of her family, she insisted that he was merely out of town on business, and that the body in the coffin was another man's.

It is not unusual for patients to deny and disavow the primary facts of illness and disease, even when previous experience might have alerted them to recurrences. One man who had coronary heart disease awakened one morning with chest pain. He then went out and bought pork sausages for breakfast. When the pain continued, he was forced to seek medical help, but he complained that his pain was due to his gall bladder, which was usually affected by eating pork sausages! He did not deny the fact of pain, but only the cause of the chest pain. Nevertheless, this was an instance of first-order denial.

Denial of clinical facts, such as chest pain, is not the same as denial of the diagnosis, but when a patient could be expected to recognize tell-tale symptoms of recurrence, it amounts to the same thing. Patients will often use words as instruments of denial, even when the word used is correct. For example, the term, "cancer," has secondary meanings that are not shared with the more euphemistic word, "tumor." Cancer, unfortunately, evokes images of decay, wasting away, corruption, and so forth. Tumor implies that the lesion is circumscribed, removable, and not apt to be very serious. Similarly, patients do not like the diagnosis of "heart attack." Instead, they may prefer to say that "something was wrong with my ticker," "the blood vessels in my heart were too narrow," or "the doctor told me that I almost had a heart attack."

Euphemisms and circumlocutions are so commonly used in medicine that it would be unfair to label anything less than calling a spade a dirty shovel an example of first- or second-order denial. Nevertheless, when clinical facts are explained by diluted diagnoses and trivial terms, it is not that a patient prefers euphemisms, but that these terms help him to avoid and nullify a recurrent threat. Gravely ill patients, for example, may explain their presence in the hospital by saying, "My doctor wants to be sure I don't have anything serious," or "I've been working too hard and need a rest."

Obviously, first-order denial precludes second- and third-order denial. When facts are negated, it is unnecessary to consider their implications.

Case 4. Although she had a large abdominal tumor that interfered with daily life, a 48-year-old housewife had minimal complaints. She complied with the treatment program, asked very few questions, and showed no apparent interest in the cause of the gross swelling. Her husband had a colostomy for bowel cancer about 20 years before. He criticized his wife's doctors for being alarmists, fools, or charlatans. The first physician she consulted attempted to be candid, but her husband became irritated and claimed that the doctor was mistaken about the diagnosis. She avoided any doctor for a long time, but then, as her tumor grew and incapacity became more pronounced, she finally found a physician who was almost unrealistically reassuring.

When hospitalization became necessary, her attitude was so inconsistent with clinical facts that a psychiatric assessment seemed obligatory. But her physician refused, fearing that the patient would become too upset. Finally, he permitted a social worker to interview the patient. To the surprise of the staff, the patient dramatically responded by pouring out her feelings about having an incurable illness. She was relieved and consoled by the interview, rather than upset. Further conversations disclosed that she had managed to keep her concern within bounds because her husband and doctor had expected denial from her, corresponding to their own reluctance to face the facts.

Case 5. After recovering from an acute myocardial infarction, a 55-year-old factory worker returned to the medical clinic regularly, but always for complaints unrelated to his heart. Then, one day, while working, severe chest pain recurred. Although it spread to his jaw, shoulder, and left arm, he did not report to a doctor for 3 days. When finally brought to the hospital, he denied suspecting that the symptoms might be another heart attack. He explained that during the first attack, the pain had extended to his fingertips. This time, however, the pain stopped at his wrist. Therefore, it could not be the same trouble he had before!

Case 6. A 52-year-old widow was being treated for two small epitheliomas. One morning she felt a lump in her breast. Instead of calling it to her doctor's attention, she waited until he was about to discharge her after treatment for the skin cancer ended. She then casually inquired if she would now be all right, not mentioning the tumor of the breast. He promptly reassured her, and the treatment was concluded. Thereafter, she avoided any contact with her affected breast, even doubling up the bath towel so she would not feel the mass. Months later, she was admitted to the hospital with extensive ulceration of her breast.

First-order denial is usually short-lived, although people may persistently minimize their symptoms throughout most of the prediagnostic period. Prediagnostic delay may be due to denial, especially when a patient has someone to help foster and encourage denial. Sometimes, it is the doctor who encourages the patient to false security. Hence, the doctor transmits first-order denial to his patient. In fairness, however, many patients hear only what they want to hear, and then protest that they had not been warned about possible qualifications and complications.

Case 7. A 65-year-old widower developed severe chest pain, but instead of calling his own physician, turned to a doctor who had erroneously minimized symptoms of cerebral thrombosis in his late wife. The doctor said that she suffered "only nerves" at the time when she was about to become paralyzed and then die. The patient later admitted that his call to the wife's physician was the first contact they had had in about seven years, so it was obvious that he preferred a doctor who would minimize his chest pain, even at the risk that another serious illness might be overlooked.

Denial of Implications

Second-order denial refers to patients who accept the primary facts of illness, even the diagnosis, but cannot visualize the implications and possible extensions of the lesion. It is reasonable, of course, to feel encouraged after a successful operation or period of convalescence, especially when a patient recovers and his doctor is reassuring. However, it is less reasonable when a patient retrospectively minimizes his illness and turns the future into a supportive set of rationalizations. For example, one man after a heart attack claimed that his heart was stronger than ever, because his doctor had compared recovery from coronary thrombosis with scar formation after a wound. "Everyone knows how tough a scar is, so my heart will be tough, too!"

Denial of implications often takes place when a patient fractionates his illness and persistent symptoms into many minor complaints, each of which can then be handled separately. As a result, the total illness cannot amount to much. Generally, patients who refuse to comment about their future and deny the possible implications of illness are seldom very optimistic. They tend to postpone specific plans on one pretext or another. Often they interpose another period of recovery between the original illness and a highly positive future. In this way, the second period is seen in more optimistic terms than if it were simply an extension of the primary disease. "Just as soon as this bleeding stops (or the wound heals, or this infection clears up), I'll be on my way!"

Case 8. A 34-year-old mother of two children had extensive treatment for breast cancer. Although she was not terminal, she could not care for herself or the children, and was tended by her widowed mother.

There was a large ulcer at the site of the mastectomy. The patient referred to this as "a tendency to infection." She avoided situations that might expose her to further infections, fearing that she might catch cold. In the hospital she insisted that her bed not be near anyone with pneumonia. Half-heartedly, she complained that "No one ever tells me anything," even though she had been told about the diagnosis and purpose of treatment. "Doctors don't tell me what is going on. I wish they would because then I'd know when I'll be well!"

Throughout her extended illness, she wove a pattern of plausible fictions around every exacerbation and complication. Many of these rationalizations concerned fear that her divorced husband would take the children away. Part of the denial was sustained by her mother, an energetic woman who had also nursed her husband and sister during their terminal illnesses. She was proud that her sister had lived for a time after doctors had given up all hope, and therefore was adamantly optimistic about her daughter. That both her husband and sister had finally died did not sway her conviction that good nursing care would prevail.

Case 9. A 37-year-old housewife, mother of three teen-aged sons, consulted a gynecologist because of uterine bleeding. In the course of the examination, a breast nodule was discovered. She was operated upon the following day, and after a biopsy showed malignancy, a mastectomy was immediately performed. Because the mutilating operation had not been anticipated, her doctor feared that the lack of preparation might cause the patient to become extremely alarmed, and possibly, suicidal. A psychiatric consultant was asked to intervene, almost as soon as the patient returned to her room.

She surprised everyone by her euphoria, and enthusiastic acceptance of the mastectomy. For several years, she had not attended church because of claustrophobia. As a devout Catholic, she feared eventual punishment. When the psychiatrist told her how fortunate she was, that the tumor was small and had been so promptly detected, she interpreted this "good fortune" as a sign of divine intercession and forgiveness.

While the staff appreciated, with relief, this highly positive response, the patient refused to return for later treatment. She insisted that God had not only forgiven her, but had performed a miracle, as well! Why would God in his goodness stop at an early diagnosis? Would he not also cure her? Therefore, she was cured. Her denial extended to other phases of life, which she idealized beyond all fact and reality. The psychiatrist knew about her serious domestic problems from her husband, but after the operation, she claimed that they had never had trouble. Follow-up psychiatric treatment was also refused. The patient would accept appointments, but then cancel, saying that she was too well to see any doctor.

Denial of Extinction

Patients may, after a time, fully accept their diagnosis, with its complications and hazards, but still resist the conclusion that incurable illness results in death. Denial of extinction resembles inability to imagine personal death, which is a sign of the primary paradox.

Third-order denial does not refer to healthy people who espouse a strong creed of immortality. It is found only among patients who have already acknowledged the facts of illness and their extensions, and face imminent confrontation with death. Aside from any philosophical and religious belief, they will behave and talk as if their present state would be indefinitely prolonged.

Case 10. A 42-year-old unmarried, practical nurse was admitted to a hospital for terminal care, about one month after she was found to have extensive abdominal metastases from carcinoma of the caecum. She had been self-supporting throughout most of her life. With the exception of a sister in a convent, she had no relatives. Her surgeon asked a social worker to arrange the transition from private life to permanent hospitalization for the patient. She accepted the diagnosis and knew the significance of the transfer, speaking frankly and without self-pity. Pain was not a prominent symptom, but she talked about not living much longer.

Several months later, the social worker received an urgent call, asking her to visit that evening. When she arrived, the patient was openly distressed, in contrast to her customary composure. The social worker and the patient had become very friendly during her hospitalization, and had spoken about death, family ties, and illness on many occasions. Now, it seemed apparent that the terminal period was about to begin. To her surprise, however, the patient said that the reason for the telephone call was to help engage a nurse to look after her when she went home. Never had the patient seemed less likely to go home or more likely to die.

It was learned that earlier that day the patient's doctor had returned from a 3-week vacation. He had little to say, and the perceptive patient realized that he was disappointed in her condition. In keeping with her policy of gentle candor, the social worker ventured to suggest that the patient was reexperiencing some of her earlier fears about dying. The patient agreed at once, recognizing the incongruity between her grave condition and plans about going home. Her distress abated promptly, and she merely commented that everyone in her situation must go through similar periods of disappointment and self-deception. Then she dropped off to sleep, but awakened to apologize for ignoring her visitor. She commented serenely that she hoped she wouldn't live much longer. After pausing a very long moment, the social worker took the patient's hand, and softly said she agreed. The woman smiled and said, "Thank you, my dear." Death occurred within 24 hours.

Denial of extinction is difficult to diagnose because it is usually assumed to be a sign of courage, hope, faith, or some other helpful attribute. However, while the patient in Case 10 showed middle knowledge briefly, the main focus of denial was death itself, not the implications of illness. Even though it occurs only at the far end of life, third-order denial is still denial because it appears only in selective situations and is communicated only to certain people with whom a patient wants to maintain a relationship. This patient wanted to spare her doctor further disappointment, and it was natural to ask her other friend, the social worker, to help her return home. But the social worker had already developed a relationship in which confrontation with death had been forthright. It was, therefore, easy for the patient to drop the denial and to accept death, once again.

DIAGNOSIS OF DENIAL

The diagnosis of first-order denial is usually simple. A sick patient has few, if any, complaints; he shows unjustified optimism or even indifference. He seems unable or unwilling to draw inferences about self-evident facts of illness.

Anyone faced with threats to survival and self-esteem is apt to call upon strategies of denial and nullification. He may say or do things that the rest of the world considers unrealistic and inappropriate. However, dogmatic classification of different types of denial is not useful, because some forms of denial exist only in the observer's mind.

Denial, like its opposite, affirmation, is grounded in biological, social, and psychological processes. Like any so-called ego function, denying entails perception, performance, symbolic forms, and interpersonal transactions. People who are abruptly exposed to external danger may freeze, close off, go dead, and then, with unnatural deliberation and calm, take steps to escape and master the threat. These are emergency situations, calling for concentration of all available energy and skills for the task. They are not instances of denial because the realistic danger is recognized and responded to appropriately and effectively. The threat is perceived; it is not negated, nor is it transformed into a more congenial reality. The ensuing behavior fits the predicament and is not incongruous. Lifton described psychological "closure" among Hiroshima survivors. Concentration camp survivors are also said to undergo chronic deadening of perceptions and emotions, as a result of their experiences. Some patients facing terminal illness may find themselves depersonalized, unable to share in the life that streams around them. Although these are examples of psychic nullification, they are not strategies that serve denial. The distinctive quality of denying and denial is that it occurs only in relation to certain people, not to all, and has the primary purpose of protecting a significant relationship.

Denial may be a personality trait of chronic optimists, or of people who are fond of "pseudo-reminiscences" that glamorize their past. Certain investigators (Rosen & Bibring, 1966) suggest that people on the "white collar" level are less likely to deny than those who are "blue collar" or "no collar." In other words, people with more to lose, with fewer resources, might deny more. This is an oversimplification because it puts the principal distinction on the basis of socioeconomic status; a better test would be the need for preserving self-esteem and significant relationships.

The dynamic interpretation of denying and denial recognizes that the investigator himself can produce denial. Articulate, educated, and prosperous patients may not be so threatened by serious illness. Their lives might not be subject to such drastic changes. More important, perhaps, is the attitude of their doctor. If he is responsive and sympathetic, he can encourage valid communication, or shut it off. The range of denial may be a monitor of any relationship. Alienation was first described among industrial workers, cut off from sources of creation and disposition. Now, however, alienation has become a favorite word, signifying disenchantment with what one has or can attain. Denial is so closely affiliated with one's values and self-image that whenever illness threatens to be a humiliating as well as an extended and incapacitating experience, denial may be expected to ensue.

Glaser and Strauss (1968) found that dying patients have either closed or open awareness of their plight. The degree of openness is not absolute. From time to time, there is selective closure and receptiveness. Often enough to be considered typical is the finding that first-order denial takes place mostly among people who are recently afflicted, and much less among the chronically ill, unless surrounding circumstances are just too much to bear. Some dying patients deny more to their earlier visitors, much less to people who remain in frequent contact. Doubt, despair, and equivocation can generate denial at any stage. The presuppositions of the observer may, indeed, prompt him to decide that denial is strong, but closer inquiry may disclose that it is the observer who has been alienated and closed off.

> *Case 11.* A middle-aged woman with severe syringomyelia seemed to be pleased when informed of her husband's death. Her behavior contrasted with the deep concern she had felt during his chronic and fatal illness, carcinoma of the lung.
>
> A consultant interviewed the patient, because it was feared that her "denial" might be the prelude of a serious depression. He discovered, however, that she did grieve for her husband, for their disrupted home, for her own invalidism. Her reaction of pleasure after his death was neither a sign of denial nor was it inappropriate. She was glad he died, because now she would not cause him additional worry when, as was inevitable, her neurological condition deteriorated. She knew about her own future. Had he lived long enough to become an invalid, she also knew that her daughters could not have left home, and might have compromised their own future.

Some professionals cannot understand that death may be both appropriate and acceptable as a solution for life's problems. Young people, insofar as they do not utterly repudiate the aged, may not believe that old people can calmly look upon death as the conclusion of a script written long ago. Therapists with "never say die" enthusiasm may diagnose depression and denial when there is no evidence of either.

The diagnosis of denial is usually decided because the reality testing used by the examiner has been violated. The preliminary process called denying, as well as its constructive dimension, is seldom heeded. The diagnosis of denial, therefore, is determined by whatever the patient and the examiner, investigator, or judge *deem to be certain*. If there is discrepancy, the weight of judgment pushes away from candid realization that, for some people, the disposition to die is more acceptable than the threat of abandonment, humiliation, loneliness.

6

Denial and Acceptance in Myocardial Infarction and Cancer

DENIAL AND ACCEPTANCE

Denial is neither a private state of mind nor an impersonal mental mechanism. Patients can be threatened in many ways, and find different means by which they can draw back, distort, or transform sources of intimidation. Although denial usually evokes images of avoidance and aversion, its full meaning cannot be grasped without also understanding its opposite, that of acceptance.

Ordinarily, denial is inferred when an outside observer believes that what a patient says or does deviates substantially from a norm. The extent of denial, however, is based upon the degree to which the patient accepts a common reality and can act upon it appropriately. Consequently, denial cannot be diagnosed without at least an implicit assessment of acceptance. Denial and acceptance are always counterpoised, so that the significance of one is automatically drawn from the appraisal of the other.

To be aware of illness is not the same as acceptance of illness. For that matter, someone who is seemingly unaware of illness is not necessarily denying. Compliance with a doctor's directions does not presuppose acceptance or awareness, nor is indifference to threats equivalent to denial of danger. These are self-evident propositions, yet according to the platitudes one hears at the bedside, patients who do not ask questions are assumed to be satisfied with their treatment and to accept their situation with equanimity. Moreover, patients who behave well and create no disturbance are considered to be aware of their doctors' efforts and deeply appreciative.

In an effort to study the relation between life-threatening illness and denial, Hackett and Weisman (1969) compared 20 patients who were hospitalized with acute myocardial infarction with 20 patients dying of cancer. From one viewpoint, these were two groups of patients who were all on the critical list because of an illness from which they might not recover. From another viewpoint, however, the study compared the responses of the staff to patients in opposite situations: terminal cancer patients were considered to be hopeless, while myocardial infarction patients were seriously ill, but had a good chance to recover.

Hope and despair are always balanced precariously when people are faced with possible death. It should not be surprising if doctors reflected despair even more readily than do patients with life-threatening illnesses, because patients, at least, have recourse to anxiety-sparing methods of mitigation, called denial. However, studies (Feder, 1966) show that professionals may deny, displace, or externalize their own concerns and anxieties, so that the ward atmosphere itself can transmit an optimistic or a pessimistic mood. Rothenberg (1961) found that when dealing with cancer patients, doctors tend to support denial, encourage isolation, discourage grief, underestimate the patient's capacity to understand, and avoid issues that threaten to disclose the doctor's loss of therapeutic control. Communication under these circumstances is always discouraged, and as a result, little information is sought or exchanged (Waxenberg, 1966).

Oken (1961) reported that some doctors justify their reluctance to be candid with dying or seriously ill patients by citing their past clinical experience, although many of the physicians he interviewed were comparative newcomers to the practice of medicine. His findings indicate that while experience is a good teacher, it needs an open mind to teach; otherwise, experience merely solidifies error and dignifies preconceptions. Oken also noted that the doctors said that even if research showed that frankness were desirable, they still might not talk freely with patients about the pessimistic side of illness.

The dispute about whether to tell or not is likely to continue, without allowing for the fact that most patients who are very ill already know more than their doctors realize. Many, if not all, sick patients want more information than their doctors are willing to share. Is candor indicated in life-threatening illnesses? When doctors decide to dissimulate and to pretend an optimism that they do not feel, can they effectively conceal their actual beliefs?

ASSUMPTIONS ABOUT MI AND CA PATIENTS

Without speaking a word, doctors and other professionals can transmit discouragement or hope, interest and concern or impersonal disdain. In the mind of the layman, that of practically all patients, the *diagnosis* of cancer is almost synonymous with a death sentence. Although a person with a heart attack may be in danger of dying, the diagnosis of myocardial infarction is seldom as threatening as that of cancer.

Patients with certain kinds of cancer have a better prognosis than many people who have sustained a heart attack, kidney disease, or advanced hypertension. Nevertheless, cancer, or CA, stands as the prototype of a disease that demands an explanation in human terms beyond medicine, as though the patient had been singled out for some special misfortune. Half of all coronary deaths occur within 24 hours of the first recognized symptoms; death rates from a second heart attack are about five times that of a first attack. Nevertheless, most myocardial infarction patients, or MI, continue to believe in their ultimate recovery, and, we must assume, given a choice between cancer with a good prognosis and myocardial infarction with the outlook it has, most people would prefer coronary thrombosis. Such is the pervasive magic of the word, cancer.

Before studying the scope of denial in MI and CA patients, Hackett and Weisman had several assumptions or working hypotheses. Because MI is generally regarded as a more hopeful illness, patients were expected to be better informed, needing little support, and to have, therefore, more opportunity to deny the threat to their life. Because CA patients in the terminal phase are so near death, it was assumed that more staff support would be required to neutralize the atmosphere of gloom. Because doctors generally favor encouraging as much denial as possible, it was assumed that doctors would tell CA patients far less in order to foster more denial. Because staff attitudes are manifestly different in dealing with CA and MI, CA patients were expected to be apprehensive and depressed, while MI patients would be, despite varying degrees of anxiety and depression, more optimistic.

In general, CA patients have more reason to deny, but because of insistent, refractory symptoms, less opportunity for it. MI patients, in contrast, might be supposed to have more opportunity to deny, but because of a more hopeful atmosphere, especially after the acute period has passed, less reason for it.

These assumptions were, admittedly, prime examples of group generalizations that could hardly fail to be borne out, provided that the individual characteristics of the patients themselves were disregarded. It was expected however that although these two populations were both dangerously ill, they would contrast in almost every other respect. Because MI patients are usually told the basic facts, and CA patients have been sick long enough to surmise a great deal without being told, few patients in either group were expected to show outright first-order denial.

METHOD OF INQUIRY

Twenty questions were devised that would focus upon situations that usually encourage denial. The questions fell into five categories: (a) what the patient is told by his doctor, (b) how the patient assimilates the information, (c) the patient's predominant concerns, fear of dying, and orientation toward the future, (d) staff-patient relationships, and (e) physical discomfort and need for medication.

MI and CA patients were matched according to age and sex. There were 14 females and 26 males, ranging in age from 27 to 74 years. Religious and socioeconomic backgrounds were essentially similar. All were on the Danger List when first interviewed. Each patient was followed by daily, weekly, or biweekly visits, depending upon the need, until discharge or death.

What Are CA and MI Patients Told?

We must understand that, although MI and CA patients are both on the Danger List and critically ill, they differ in the way they become ill and in the degree of recovery each can expect. CA patients were sick for a long time before they were admitted to the hospital. MI patients, in contrast, were usually working or reasonably active until the very day of admission. Consequently, the cardiac patient is encouraged in his hope for partial recovery, at least, and he is supported in his efforts to deny the more pessimistic aspects of illness. Moreover, the disposition to deny is favored by acuteness of onset.

The CA patient is less likely to respond favorably to denial, even though he may ask few questions and appear to be unaware of his plight. He has been accustomed to illness and treatment, and as a rule, has accommodated himself to progressive limitations.

These considerations are essential to a more comprehensive appreciation that *what* CA and MI patients are told is determined by intangible factors, such as what the doctor himself believes and is willing to say, and the way in which information or, for that matter, non-information is transmitted.

Naturally enough, doctors tend to be open, reticent, and guarded in dealing with their patients. Presumably, no one, including physicians, can be utterly frank at all times, nor is anyone totally guarded in speaking about every topic related to illness. As a result, there is no reliable method to determine what is actually told to patients and how much is assimilated. Hackett and Weisman had fairly accurate impressions, supported by the informal agreement of colleagues, about which doctors were candid, considerate, brusque, or ultra-professional. They spoke directly with each physician about his patient, but what these doctors reported telling the patient was always open to doubt. Few human beings, especially professionals, will readily admit to not liking someone else, especially when that person is a patient, nor will they acknowledge that their comments carry a negative connotation.

For rating purposes, it was decided that when a physician gave minimal information and made no effort to elicit and answer questions, his reticence was probably associated with very incomplete information. In contrast, when the doctor told his patient about the diagnosis, proposed treatment, and anticipated course, this was considered to be full and candid information. Between these extremes were the doctors who gave incomplete or very qualified and selected information.

While this rating plan is practical, it is only realistic to realize that some doctors believe they are always open and frank, but their comments are so technical and truncated that further discussion is precluded. Doctors may respond quite appropriately, and feel that they are supportive in what they say, but their true attitudes may be revealed in nonverbal ways or in speaking about seemingly unrelated topics. For example, a physician might tell his patient about the diagnosis, without elaborating or explaining the implications and possible extensions of the disease. His own second-order "denial" would then lead him to treat his patient's cough, say, as if it were unrelated to the primary disease. His manner creates a split between what he says and what he does, thereby fostering more denial than he supposes. On the other hand, another doctor might be more consistent and explain symptoms as part of the general condition as a whole.

It is unreasonable to expect closed or open awareness throughout a patient's illness. Reticence in one situation may alternate with candor in another. No doctor would claim that he was unavailable to his patients; most doctors, when specifically asked, say that they are willing to answer questions, but that no questions arise. They assume that patients who do not ask for more information are satisfied, which, of course, they may well be, although silence is not necessarily equivalent to satisfaction.

It was confirmed that CA patients are not told the full truth about illness as often as MI patients. Only 7 of the 20 CA patients were given ample information, 3 patients were told little or nothing, and 10 were given very meager facts about themselves. Nevertheless, when queried by the psychiatrists, 15 CA patients had a reasonably clear idea about their illness, including the diagnosis and outlook. Only 5 patients seemed relatively unaware of what was happening. Because all of the CA patients had been treated extensively in the hospital before the present admission, these findings suggest that when CA patients fail to ask pertinent questions or seem "satisfied" or apathetic about incomplete information, it is because there is really no need to ask. The disparity between what doctors tell CA patients and what the patients actually know already tends, therefore, to increase during the terminal period. However, a few doctors were surprised that patients knew so much, while others, even reticent doctors who told little, assumed that patients were already aware of the grim facts.

Seventeen MI patients were given full information; three received incomplete information, and none were told nothing at all about their illness. Moreover, information was transmitted in generally optimistic terms, in contrast to reluctant, equivocal communications between doctors and CA patients.

How Do CA and MI Patients Assimilate Information?

This question was answered by observing how patients tended to accept hospitalization, and how they responded to facts of illness. Did the patient ever speak about death? Was he thought to be depressed, anxious, or essentially "normal" in mood? Did he ever speak about fear, discouragement, loneliness? Did he seem to understand what was said to him, and to accept the limitations of illness?

Judging by the questions asked by patients, there was no significant difference in attitudes toward respective limitations, even though these limitations of illness varied between groups. Of 20 MI patients, 11 did not seem to assimilate information fully. Nine patients were willing to talk about a remote future, but not about day-by-day uncertainty. This was thought to be a sign of second-order denial; they accepted and assimilated the fact of having had a heart attack, but not all the limitations and risks that such a diagnosis entailed.

Nine CA patients seemed wholly disinterested in any future, remote or at hand. This might be construed as an attitude compatible with simply being very sick and not caring, but it might also indicate that they had come to terms with their own terminality.

What Are Their Predominant Concerns, Fear of Dying, and Orientation toward the Future?

CA patients were aware that death was in their immediate future; 11 were able to speak of it spontaneously. Fourteen

MI patients knew that their lives were in danger during the acute period, and remained aware of critical illness throughout hospitalization. Only one patient in each group expressed a direct fear of dying.

According to the staff observers, only two CA patients had "normal" mood; the others were thought to be quite depressed. In contrast, the staff assessed 14 MI patients as "normal." When the psychiatrists asked patients about depression, anxiety, and general uneasiness, nine CA patients denied being troubled, three MI patients readily admitted depression, anxiety, or uneasiness, eight MI patients reluctantly reported these feelings, and nine MI patients denied them. In short, the same number of MI patients and CA patients denied depression, anxiety, or uneasiness. While there was considerable difference in the explicit moods of the MI and CA patients, it was not as great as the staff thought.

The two groups differed in their predominant concerns. Eighteen CA patients were worried lest their symptoms could not be controlled or relieved. No cardiac patient was concerned about this. Eleven MI patients were primarily concerned about their ability to return to work, and five patients claimed they had no fear whatsoever.

It was almost incredible that only one patient in each group volunteered that he was afraid of dying. Were we to accept this finding, it would mean that MI patients were so supported that no fears were possible, and that CA patients had come to terms so completely with their outlook that fear of dying belonged to the past, not to the present. It seems more reasonable, in the light of the substantial number of patients in each group who denied depression, anxiety, and uneasiness, to regard absence of explicit fear of dying as an artifact of observation, not a reliable indication of concern. We are already familiar with patients who tangentially voice misgivings about recovery, couching their comments in semifacetious terms, gratuitously talking about their relief and reassurance. These patients are seldom thought to be particularly worried, and it is the rare clinician who probes their facade. Nevertheless, grim humor, magnification of faint improvement, forced optimism, casual references to friends with fatal illnesses, and recollections of past misfortunes overcome may be allusions to predominant concerns that neither the patient nor his doctor is prepared to recognize. When directly interrogated, few patients admit worry, but often there are gaps between what a patient feels, what he can put into words, what he is willing to report, what staff observers see, and what they deem worth remembering and recording.

It is likely that there were still situations in which patients belonging to both groups might have been inconspicuously concerned and worried. When patients were interviewed at length, CA patients tended to be more concerned about enforced separation from family and friends than about impending death. As a group, MI patients worried about their ability to continue work and be self-supporting. Despite surface confidence, at least half of the MI patients had reservations about their independence and productivity in the future. On the other hand, CA patients had been sick for so long that to express concern about returning to work would have been a sign of denial. As a group, CA patients were on a level of survival for its own sake. Their hope was to control pain and discomfort. If they visualized a productive future, their plans were considered "unrealistic." When allowance was made for the difference in "unrealistic plans" for MI and CA patients, an equal number of patients entertained future plans that were inconsistent with their physical status.

How Do Staff-Patient Relationships Differ?

Reciprocal responses of staff and patients are always difficult to assess. Doctors tend to report findings that accord with their expectations in the psychological domain. Patients often respond in the way that people expect. Differences are usually submerged. Hospital charts tell us little about this, and verbal reports seldom divulge negative attitudes. Moreover, some patients can be exceedingly difficult, but do not elicit staff antagonism. Other patients can be extremely cooperative, yet be virtually ignored; still other patients can be very demanding, even outrageous, and yet be very popular with the staff. Hostility is easy to conceal at times, but at other times insists upon leaving its traces.

With these precautions in mind, it was found that five CA patients complained frequently about the staff, six occasionally complained, and nine never complained. Only one MI patient complained occasionally, none complained frequently, and every MI patient was said to be "liked" by the staff! Because they were said to be demanding and unappreciative, four CA patients were frankly disliked, while five other patients and their families tended to court hostility.

Only one MI patient was said to have asked for reassurance, while seven CA patients significantly sought reassurance from the staff, even though the staff believed that almost every CA patient was disturbed or depressed. Eleven MI patients had qualms and doubts about their ability to go back to work, but did not seek reassurance for this.

The dearth of reported requests for reassurance could mean several things: (a) There was little communication beyond everyday talk about illness, (b) MI patients were adequately reassured soon after admission, so that further requests were unnecessary, (c) the ward atmosphere was sufficiently reassuring in itself, (d) occasional bids for reassurance might have been too slight to notice, (e) CA patients were mainly concerned about physical symptoms; other appeals for reassurance were superfluous, and (f) when patients realize that they are being treated well, they will not ask for additional reassurance.

What are the Differences in Physical Distress and Need for Medication?

CA patients asked for and received more medication and derived less relief than did MI patients, a finding that is not only obvious but helps to explain why medication was the chief topic of concern for CA patients. Furthermore, when relief of symptoms is only partial, disagreements about the type, dose, and frequency of medication may lead to broader tensions between the patient and staff.

While open friction between staff and patient is seldom reported, indirect indications could be obtained by asking about the physician's attitude toward giving a patient ample medication. In this area, physicians may disclose an ambivalence that they would hesitate to express directly. Patients are encouraged to follow the explicit and implicit rules of a hospital and of the special ward. It is, as a rule, the doctor who decides about the nature and dose of any medication; patients risk disapproval, at least, should they ask for more. Alienation induced by such tacit disapproval might, therefore, account for the apparent absence of overt anxiety and bids for reassurance. When doctors assert that they have successfully strengthened denial in CA patients, it may be because very sick and helpless patients are reluctant to complain. The paramount problem, as the end approaches, is to find just that amount of medication which relieves pain but will not create additional problems. When death is at hand, few doctors withhold ample medication.

SUMMARY

It was originally assumed that MI patients would have more opportunities to deny, and that CA patients had more reason to deny. Our actual findings were that neither group had an edge on the other so far as denial was concerned. The optimistic staff attitude did not create collective denial or universal optimism among MI patients. The situation was more obscure for CA patients, because the staff had split attitudes about information, anxiety, mood disturbances, complaints, and medication. Very little was said to CA patients, but it is possible that considerably more communication took place than was reported.

Almost every staff member thought that CA patients were disturbed in some way, but most discussions turned on the general topic of medication, not upon explaining and anticipating physical deterioration or death. Conversely, the staff consensus was that MI patients were hopeful and did not need further reassurance. Actually, inquiry disclosed that many MI patients had misgivings about how much recovery and return to function they could expect.

Contrary to expectations, the MI and CA populations were not opposites. They had similar concerns which were masked by realistic differences in prognosis, in need for medication, and in the availability of a supportive doctor-patient relationship. The actual incidence of denial was still difficult to determine. CA patients knew much about their true condition, but did not voluntarily speak about it, nor was the staff readily available. MI patients were told a great deal, but efforts to encourage denial did not wholly obliterate worry and anxiety.

We can summarize the findings by noting that denial is always difficult to enforce, and that acceptance may be a more practical alternative. Indeed, did patients do as well as they did because doctors encouraged denial or because they already had a capacity for acceptance which could not be counteracted? Acceptance is far easier to achieve than is denial. After a chronic illness has taken hold, blanket denial is virtually impossible, unless the doctor urges the patient to relinquish reality testing as well.

This study also suggested that hope and despair do not wholly depend upon realistic considerations, such as the diagnosis, prognosis, or critical stage of acute illness. There is no certain method for assessing the proportion of denial or acceptance that anyone actually experiences. Denial and acceptance do vary in the course of illness, and do not seem tied to a special diagnosis or to a selective environment. It is or should be axiomatic that without open communication, there can be nothing but conjecture. Categorical edicts about what any patient should be told, how he ought to behave, and what will bolster hope pertain to stereotypes, not to people.

The disposition to deny (and to accept) is decided by many intangible factors which have a qualitative reality, but defy our efforts to measure and count. Cross-sectional comparison of different diagnostic populations, even though both are threatened with death, shows that there is still no reliable index about what goes on within the individual. Patients with an illness carrying a good prognosis may deny more persistently than do patients in whom death is inevitable.

Any dying patient is aware that time is running out, whether or not people looking after him are willing to acknowledge it. During the course of a threatening illness, shifts in the mixture of denial and acceptance are something like sand flowing down an hourglass. At first, during the initial period, there are both reasons for optimism and opportunities for denial. Then, as will be described in Chapter 7, first-order denial decreases and, falling to the bottom, becomes first-order acceptance. Time goes on, and according to the progressive encounter with inexorable illness, second-order denial passes into second-order acceptance. Then, when inimical forces exhaust reasonable means of denial, even third-order denial yields to acceptance, and the sands run out (Figure 1).

3rd Order Denial
2nd Order Denial
1st Order Denial

3rd Order Acceptance
2nd Order Acceptance
1st Order Acceptance

FIGURE 1. Time runs out.

7

Death from a Fatal Illness:
Cancer

We only ask what something "means" when direct perception and immediate experience are neither self-evident nor self-fulfilling. In that case, the event is referred to something beyond what is present and perceived. Sickness is a confusing occasion, because it is so difficult to find a reason that gives a meaning to sickness. The perception of sickness is certainly self-evident, but it is a self-defeating, not a self-fulfilling, experience. The discomfort and disability entailed by being sick in the here-and-now discourage investigation or even interest in meaning. Fortunately, however, most people who are sick know that they will soon be restored to good health. If they can be relieved of discomfort, they will not seek to understand why they have been singled out to be ill.

The meaning of illness becomes more pertinent when sickness is extended and involves helplessness and the threat of death. Survival may itself be uncertain. Effective performance within a familiar orbit of activity is drastically, and perhaps permanently compromised. The afflicted patient

95

must, therefore, assess his place in the world. He asks himself what has happened, where he is going, what he can expect, what it all means. The past is irretrievable, the future is uncertain. He is forced to relinquish his customary expectation that life will go on indefinitely. He must revise reality; his options are curtailed; his self-image is transformed.

Adaptation to serious illness follows the steps already described for denying and denial: (a) *Recognition* of a reality, (b) *repudiation* of a threatening portion, (c) *replacement* with a more congenial, tolerable meaning, and, finally, (d) *reorientation* to the changes. In short, there is recognition of a painful meaning, or reality, "I might die," obligatory yielding, even capitulation to some inexorable fact, then resolution of conflict, and reconstitution. When the problem entails adaptation to a *fatal* illness, an afflicted person must reorient himself by coping with the meaning and fact of personal extinction.

In Chapter 6, MI and CA patients were compared with respect to denial and acceptance, within the context of the hospital and staff attitudes. The results showed that cross-sectional matching of patients according to the diagnosis did not reveal the very personal significance of being sick and threatened by death. Diagnosis allows us to compare patients only with impersonal information. The more precise the data, furthermore, the less relevant the information seemed to be for each individual.

In this chapter, we shall follow the longitudinal method of comparing one patient with another. What changes does the person undergo when he becomes ill with a fatal disease? What happens during the stage of discovery, diagnosis, treatment, relapse, and final deterioration? What physical and emotional complications arise? We can assume only that as illness progresses, the person who is the patient will change.

The vital medium of existence will be altered according to the fields and forces that act upon him.

The path from *primary recognition* of disease to *incipient death* is highly idiosyncratic. Only when we stand at a distance does human behavior seem subject to laws and to prediction. Nevertheless, it is possible to recognize and describe general phases of fatal illness, without imposing sterility or an artificial stereotyped version of threatening events.

We must first distinguish between longitudinal *organic changes*, called the course of the disease, and *psychosocial stages* of fatal illness. Organic changes depend upon the biology of disease, its invasiveness, rate of development, sensitivity to treatment, site of involvement, potential for recurrence, and so forth. While organic changes create many personal and social changes in the life-space and style of an afflicted patient, psychosocial stages follow a sequence that is not determined wholly by physical factors.

When we think about fatal illness, cancer is the disease that first comes to mind. This does not mean that other illnesses can be ignored. Obviously, people can die from many causes, and the person with a diagnosis of cancer does not live with a fatal prognosis in every case. Although we cannot have foreknowledge of what anyone's death certificate will say, we must recognize the psychosocial reality that, to most people, cancer is a paradigm of fatal disease. Research and treatment continue to be encouraging, but the *diagnosis* itself has grim and persistent implications that prejudice our judgments of what being sick with cancer implies.

Few doctors are rash enough to pronounce any cancer patient "cured," even though many people return to productive and rewarding lives, and for practical purposes, consider themselves recovered from illness. From the viewpoint of internal reality, however, even the recovered patient may legitimately wonder if his good health means eradication of disease, or only a temporary reprieve.

Cancer patients who have not recovered completely have even more qualms. Despite partial return of function and intermittent good health, there is always a threat of further relapses, disabilities, and symptoms, regardless of denial. Final decline may, of course, be years away, but many cancer patients discover that in the midst of good health, the specter of inevitable and inexorable death always hovers nearby. Thus, if fate seems so predetermined, albeit indefinite, we can expect distinctive social and emotional problems to arise at different phases of illness. Moreover, appropriate resolution of these psychosocial problems may be necessary at every stage in order to assure a harmonious acceptance of the outcome.

PSYCHOSOCIAL STAGES

Three phases of personal response to the course of fatal illness are distinctive enough to be called psychosocial stages. These stages are I, *Primary Recognition*, II, *Established Disease*, and III, *Final Decline*. Subgroups of each stage can also be described, but for present purposes, might obscure our understanding of the longitudinal sequences.

Stage I, Primary Recognition, covers the period from a patient's first awareness that something is amiss to the time of the definitive diagnosis. Stage II, Established Disease, is an intermediate phase which embraces events between a patient's initial response to the diagnosis and his reactions prior to the onset of the terminal period. Stage II also pertains to the periodicity of illness, its relapses, remissions, progress, and periods of arrest. Stage III, Final Decline, begins when a patient undergoes unmistakable decline towards death. It ends when death is at hand.

Each stage presents different degrees of denial and acceptance. First-order denial of the *diagnosis* is found during Stage I and early Stage II. Second-order denial of *extensions and implications of illness* is common in Stage II. Second- and third-order denial of *fatal outcome* is typical during Stage III, often persisting until the very end. When we compared orders of denial in cancer patients, 80% of Stage I patients expressed first- or second-order denial, while only 35% of Stage III patients failed to accept the diagnosis or extensions of illness, even when they had not previously been interviewed with this purpose in mind. In other words, 65% of cancer patients realized that they had an illness from which they might never recover. Understandably enough, only 20% of Stage I patients were pessimistic about the outcome. Many cancer patients will report having a quasi-premonition about a fatal disease, but they still tend to deny the diagnosis or implications of illness, and hope that on this occasion, their omen will not be fulfilled.

The problems that beset cancer patients at each stage can best be described by assessing the degree of denial and acceptance. Stage I shows trends that may be called *denial and postponement*. Stage II which deals with vicissitudes of established disease is typified by *mitigation and displacement* of concerns about death. Stage III which foreshadows death itself presents problems of *counter-control and cessation*. During final decline, the goal of treatment is no longer that of cure, but of relief. With the approach of death, a patient must stay closer to sources of help. As the life-line shortens, autonomy and self-esteem become compromised. Despite reassurances of others, a patient's choices, control, and alternatives for sustaining his functional significance are drastically curtailed. He must, therefore, yield his own control to the counter-control of others.

PRELIMINARY ATTITUDES TOWARDS DEATH

Psychosocial stages are permeated with signs of the primary paradox. Man accepts the reality of organic and objective death, but cannot imagine his own extinction. Consequently, despite obvious depletion and deterioration, most patients still cling to an image of survival which promises to preserve their unique, distinctive *consciousness*.

The ancient Egyptians created extensions of temporal life by constructing elaborate tombs filled with objects and symbols of everyday life. We, too, find it impossible to imagine a world that will not feel our *presence* in some way. Indeed, it is *absence*, not merely physically but emotionally and symbolically, that makes death so meaningless for the individual. Fine talk about perpetuation of the species or endurance of our artifacts provides but little solace for this blunt fact, that we will be gone, extinct, and might as well have never been.

The desire to perpetuate our presence and to ensure our continuity may be expressed in specific forms through yearning for extensions of person, possessions, pursuits, or influences. Patients in Stage III may involve themselves in a relentless search for a life-saving miracle, grasping at new remedies and new physicians. Or they may turn to exotic philosophies that encourage belief in the unreality of death. How intensely the pursuit is followed depends upon how intently denial is maintained in conjunction with the primary paradox. Here, of course, the question of death and religion should be raised. Religion recognizes man's yearning for survival and depends upon man's inability to imagine anything else. Most religious viewpoints, I think, are based upon three versions of death and, by implication, survival. These are (a) metamorphosis, (b) restoration, and (c) extinction.

Metamorphosis is a belief in *rebirth* following physical death, but without consciousness of a previous existence. Continuity, thus assured, even without recollection, becomes a kind of perpetual presence, an outcome which seems more desirable than total obliteration. *Restoration* is a viewpoint that proclaims another life after death, but one in which recollection is retained. The belief that *extinction* follows life is not really as nihilistic as it appears. Its exponents state that they have no knowledge of anything located beyond the grave. But they may also claim that personal continuity is guaranteed by means of their good works, exemplary behavior, ethical standards, and so forth. The implication of this viewpoint is that personal presence is preserved through what one does or represents. It is, in effect, a derivative survival through one's principles and artifacts. The logical fourth version of death would be that of unequivocal *annihilation*, which is the antithesis of religion and of hoped-for survival. Other than in existential pronouncements, this opinion seems to have few organized supporters.

These three viewpoints are found in most creeds and eschatologies. Cultural diversity and theological minutiae may conceal the basic fact that man is concerned about his individual consciousness and personal presence. Even the view that we have no recollection of what went on before birth and no sure awareness of what will follow death still seeks to preserve some kind of being, despite death. For all we know, this might be an after-life! And there are equally cogent reasons and equally persuasive non-reasons for anticipating another such miracle in the future.

It is certainly beyond my scholarship and the purposes of this book to dwell upon various religious orientations and reconstitutions about death. However, *metamorphosis, restoration*, and *extinction* match the three psychosocial stages I have postulated: *denial and postponement, mitigation and displacement*, and *counter-control and cessation*.

At first, patients repudiate awareness and postpone action. This corresponds to a theory of death which denies dying, and therefore recognizes only the enduring quality of life. Later on, patients may acknowledge the diagnosis, but not the extensions and implications of fatal illness. This resembles a theory of death in which, having died, life is restored. Finally, when death is at hand, patients may accept the reality of fatal illness, yet repudiate total annihilation. By yielding control to the benevolent dispositions and memories of survivors, they manage to live on. In all theories of death, we die, but some token evidence of our life still testifies to our abiding presence.

STAGE I. DENIAL AND POSTPONEMENT

Unless we happen to be the afflicted person, doctors learn about the primary abnormalities that first bring people to an awareness of something amiss only through retrospective means. Cancer patients, for example, usually consult doctors because they have observed one or more of the so-called seven cardinal signs: bleeding, swelling, weight loss, bowel changes, and so forth. There may also be nonspecific, systemic signs of underlying illness, such as sleep disturbance, unusual fatigue, appetite loss, and other perceptions that interfere only slightly with everyday life. Delay in seeking diagnosis is influenced by the invisibility of a specific lesion, its inconstancy, its symptomless location, or any other factors preventing early detection. Some people do consult their doctors promptly, but many others delay, postpone, rationalize, and find still further reasons to blunt awareness and action. Sutherland (1960) reported that delay occurs both with tumors of low malignancy and with highly invasive, rapidly growing lesions. Physicians, who should know better, tend to ignore primary signs of cancer in themselves and in their patients. Well-educated people do not seek diagnosis earlier than others, suggesting that it is not simple ignorance that explains delay in diagnosis. Conspicuous lesions and incapacitating symptoms are quite compatible with first-order denial (Moses & Cividali, 1966).

According to retrospective reports, patients often turn first to friends, not for guidance but for reassurance. Among more common tactics are self-medication, optimistic rationalizations, selective disregard, and avoidance of whatever might be a reminder of serious illness. And, with the inconsistency of anyone who is in conflict, the same person who carefully shuns newspaper articles about illness will often compare his own worrisome symptoms with the accounts of illness that he hears discussed in his presence.

Stage I combines an "out of sight, out of mind" attitude with a growing sense of vulnerability. Men are more apt to postpone diagnosis than are women, in part because threatening symptoms and signs in men are less conspicuous. Stage III men, we found, delayed seeking help longer than women did, and as a result, the disease was already advanced when finally diagnosed. A positive family history does not facilitate earlier diagnosis. Some people delay simply because they are fatalistic and resigned. However, it may turn out that resignation and fatalism are only convenient disguises for denial; when the diagnosis of cancer is made, these patients may deny extensions and implications as adamantly as anyone else.

It has been observed that delay and postponement in early cancer may not be shortened through public educational programs (Goldsen, 1963; Lynch & Krush, 1968). Many people will break off friendships with anyone who is gravely ill, rather than expose themselves to a threatened diagnosis. Even hypochondriacal patients who have constantly feared and been convinced that they harbor malignant diseases will shun tests when they suspect that an organic disease really exists. Some people who consulted doctors report that, when the primary signs of cancer appeared, they postponed visits to their physician, even when scheduled.

Denial can be diagnosed with more confidence when patients actually pretend that manifest lesions do not exist. This does not require "negative hallucinations." People may avoid social contacts so that their changed appearance will not be commented upon. A man with a persistent cough, for example, may give up the theater or church; a woman will strategically avoid touching her breast; another patient with rectal bleeding will make sure that he does not look in the toilet bowl. People seek a "psychosomatic" diagnosis for unexplained weight loss, lack of appetite, or insomnia, even though they might have scorned a recommendation that they see a psychiatrist under other circumstances. Indeed, it is not always easy to differentiate psychosocial stress from early symptoms of almost any illness. Schmale (1964), and Engel (1967, 1968) have described how physical illness often arises from situations in which a patient gives up or feels given up. Parkes (1970), too, has found that somatic illness frequently develops after the death of someone close to the patient.

While denial and postponement are characteristic of Stage I patients, there are other people who do not deny, but report strong premonitions about developing fatal illness. They delay and postpone, lest their convictions be confirmed or nullified. These uneasy forebodings come from external sources, such as an evil spell or curse, or from internal beliefs, such as a conviction of guilt and expectation of punishment. Moreover, the onset of premonitory symptoms may coincide with an anniversary date, especially one marking an important transition period or a serious loss (Aitken-Swan & Easson, 1959).

Case 12. A 70-year-old retired craftsman entered the hospital because of severe abdominal pain. He complained bitterly, threatening suicide if the pain could not be relieved. He announced that the pain was due to cancer of the liver, and that his son had died of the same disease, precisely six years before, to the day.

As a young man, he had been in frequent trouble with the police because of drinking and brawling. On two occasions he was hospitalized with delirium tremens. However, at age 36, he suddenly stopped drinking, found a steady job, studied at night, and became a model citizen in his home community. His daughters also became exemplary women. They all married substantial husbands, raised their families without incident, and rewarded their father with honor and pride. Indeed, the patient's only enduring problem was his son, who drank excessively, neglected his wife and family, consorted with loose women, and, at age 37, was hospitalized with the diagnosis of alcoholic psychosis. One year later, while still a patient in the hospital, he died of cancer of the liver.

The patient was a forceful, articulate, patriarchal person who expounded his views eloquently during pain-free periods. "We are born and we die, that's all there is. It's a law of nature that we can't fight. Nothing can be changed. All any man can do is to fight adversity, but he must die!" He did not grieve, but accepted the inevitability of death. He regarded his son's death as a tragedy. While he brooded, he did not openly mourn.

All diagnostic tests were equivocal. When his pain diminished somewhat, so that it looked as if his prediction about incipient death might not be correct, the patient became more depressed. He was sent home, to return for follow-up study.

One week after discharge, he returned to the emergency ward with a recurrence of abdominal pain. He was certain that this time, he would die. For the next 3 days, his long-delayed mourning for his son came to the surface. He shifted between strong vituperations against himself and against his son; he raged at the futility of his son's life. It was difficult to decide whom he hated, as though he and his son were but one. On the fourth hospital day, still complaining of abdominal pain, he suddenly died.

Autopsy revealed widespread lymphomatosis, with extensive lesions in the liver. Physicians were still baffled by the extent of the disease, with so little to show on physical examination. Nevertheless, his death fulfilled the augury, the diagnosis, the identification of the patient with his dead son.

After his death, the major facts were found to be as the patient reported. Until one month prior to admission, he had been asymptomatic. The pains began within 24 hours of the son's death, six years earlier. There was scarcely any denial in this instance, but he evidently postponed seeking a diagnosis until the anniversary when his symptoms started. Fatalism, in this case, found a biological counterpart.

Self-deception is a common human trait; so, too, is a belief in fatalism and in being an exception. Opposite attitudes may serve a similar purpose, that of shielding us against fully realizing our own vulnerability. For example, lung cancer is one of the few malignancies that we can help prevent, and cancer prevention is certainly a well-publicized cause, which everyone supports. Yet, despite the hazard, comparatively few adults give up smoking. They recognize the risk, but follow the psychology of fatalism and of being the exception. Nothing can prevent a disaster, if it is going to happen, and, besides, I will be the exception. Automobile accidents happen to someone else, and there is nothing I can do to prevent someone from running into me. Self-deception prompts us to proclaim, with bravado, that we will all die sometime of something, but this statement also implies that we always expect to die of something else. Case 12 deceived no one, except, possibly, his doctors. Not only did he expect to die, but he predicted both the occasion and the cause.

Case 13. A 54-year-old tailor smoked regularly since adolescence. Even after a serious myocardial infarction when he was 48, he continued to smoke excessively, declaring that if it was his fate to die, nothing could be done about it. At age 50, he ignored the early signs of epidermal carcinoma of the tongue, not even finding out if the lesion could be treated. Later, when it was found that the cancer had spread to regional lymph nodes, he was not alarmed. He had expected the worst, and it had happened. He was prepared to die. His negligence seemed to have an inner purpose, like the pessimist who arranges to fail so that he will never be disappointed.

STAGE II. MITIGATION AND DISPLACEMENT

Until a diagnosis is made, every person, any potential patient, is alone with his uncertainty. If he delays and postpones, anxiety will mount, even though tactics of avoidance and denial seem to offer shelter. When he finally sees a doctor, that fact alone will reduce his secret terror, because he has shared concern with someone else. Still, he now starts another phase, requiring adjustments that may extend over months and years.

The private events between the time of diagnosis and the final decline are not revealed in the dry statistics of tables and charts. Denial and acceptance shift during the course of illness, according to deployment of defenses, encroachment of disease, and changes in the psychosocial field.

No patient is typical. Only representative responses, true for many people, can be described. While Stage II responses are those that show mitigation and displacement, there are problems related to the initial diagnosis and treatment, called *initial responses,* problems caused by vicissitudes of illness, called *intermediate responses*, and problems induced by the onset of final decline, called *preterminal responses*.

Initial Responses

Case 14. A 58-year-old mother of two grown daughters refused to allow mastectomy for cancer of the breast. Although she had had two benign breast tumors removed in the past, she protested that amputation of her breast would decrease her desirability as a woman. She explained that 13 years earlier, while on a trip to Europe, she had a shipboard romance with a married man whose wife was said to be an invalid. He had refused to continue the affair, but she still hoped that circumstances would one day permit them to marry.

The initial response to the diagnosis of cancer and to the surgical treatment was based entirely upon this fantasied romance. The threat to her life was not important. When the psychiatrist realized that she was firm about her refusal, he said that regardless of what might happen in the future, she would not be much good to her erstwhile friend if she were dead. Besides, he might even want her to have the operation. The patient then made an overseas telephone call to this man whom she had known so briefly. We have no record of his answer; he might not have recalled their meeting. Nevertheless, he heard her out, then advised her to do what the doctors suggested. Reassured by his apparent interest, she agreed to undergo surgery.

This is an unusual response only because it is taken out of context. Contrary to expectations, many people do not become panicky, fearing for their life. Instead, they become nostalgic about the past, recalling missed opportunities, options not taken, people long absent. They may remember the death of someone close to them in the past, or summon up the substance of a fantasy that sustains them, as with this patient. The initial response, in brief, may be remorse, or it may be a kind of shudder when faced with relinquishing unfulfilled dreams. At other times, the initial response may simply revive memories of better days.

Case 15. A 75-year-old widow opposed amputation of her foot for bone cancer, insisting that the lesion was not cancer, but a "stubborn infection." Actually, the "stubbornness" was appropriate in a way, because her derisive and depressed attitude covered bitter disappointment about life in general. Gradually, she revealed that the proposed operation not only would impose a severe physical handicap but would, once and for all, cut her off from the tranquillity and loved people she had known.

In her youth she had been a professional vaudevillean, dancing and singing, until her retirement after marriage. She had two sons, one of whom was killed in World War II, while the other, also a veteran, became a drifter and had not been heard from in many years. Her husband had died many years before of a heart attack.

She was understandably bitter about the past and hopeless about the future, but she responded somewhat to the doctor's genuine interest in her former life. She turned out to be a rather colorful person who had a knack for the anecdote, especially when speaking of well-known theatrical people of another era. She even showed the doctor the few mementoes that remained, and one day, let him see the medal that her son had been posthumously awarded for gallantry. On the day after, she relinquished her claim that the cancer was only a stubborn infection, and then spoke with sorrow about her other son. She felt abandoned, but wondered if he were still living somewhere. It became clear that for this former dancer and devoted mother, amputation would be cutting off the past entirely, a final capitulation to inexorable necessity. Nothing would be left but to complete her life in solitude. Then, surprisingly, she reported that she had been born only a short distance from the hospital, so that, in a way, the proposed surgery meant a return to where she had begun. She considered the operation to be a closing of the circle, rather than another disappointment and tragedy. The intangible and the physical losses came together now; she agreed to the amputation, tolerated it well, and then accepted placement in a suitable nursing home.

Kubler-Ross (1969) has outlined a series of common responses to learning about a fatal diagnosis. Anger, fear, depression, resentment, relief are all found from time to time, not necessarily in a predictable sequence. Shock and surprise usually come first. The "Who, me?" gives way to the "Why me?" when the patient realizes, as if for the first time, that everyone is mortal, and no one is an exception. Dejection may be followed by resentment about an unjust, hostile fate. But, because it is difficult to resent fate and impersonal necessity, anger may be displaced to a doctor who did not insist upon a searching investigation or definitive treatment. In a more magical sense, some patients feel betrayed because the doctor proved not to be infallible, and did not protect them against calamity. The displacement may be so extreme that the patient may be called "paranoid." However, the projected anger is not pathological, but rather an existential "paranoia" about the indifference of powers beyond control and conciliation. Some patients decide that the diagnosis and the disease are a punishment for a by-gone, even unspecified offense. Others feel that life has duped them again. One woman who had been struck in her breast while interceding in a family fight blamed her son and husband for causing breast cancer. While prior injuries can seldom be the cause of cancer, it is not unusual for patients to see a connection between a deadly illness and a "stroke of fate," having symbolic significance. Another woman believed, for example, that carcinoma of the cervix had been caused by her ex-husband who abandoned her and married her "closest friend." These recondite meanings usually characterize the guilty parties as "dearest" or "closest" to them, as if deception is more painful, or carries greater magic when it comes from a "beloved enemy." We can be betrayed only by someone we love, and there are some situations in which only revenge is an appropriate response.

Initial responses are more intense when the illness is more than a physical threat, and amounts to a social catastrophe. For a young father, cancer is a greater disaster than it is for an elderly bachelor. Hinton reports that most anguish and intense pain tend to occur in younger men who develop cancer before they have really established themselves as adults. Their children are young, they have debts, their wives are not equipped to carry the burden of raising dependent children. The wife, too, may feel betrayed, and in some instances, blame her husband for foreaking her. The suicide risk is often greater among younger cancer victims, possibly because professionals and other concerned people are so appalled and feel so helpless. The element of magic is seldom missing in any patient, however, leading the patient to feel that there is a connection between fatal illness and other kinds of misfortunes and despair.

Intermediate Responses

Case 16 illustrates both initial and intermediate responses. The contrast between these helps to point up the developmental pattern of patient reactions.

> *Case 16.* A 75-year-old former carpenter was certain that a melanoma under his left thumbnail came from multiple injuries, even though he had not worked at his trade for over five years. The left thumb is indispensable to a carpenter, so when the surgeon recommended amputation, the patient reacted as though he had done something to get himself fired from a job.
>
> His initial response was to feel that once again he had failed. He talked about being out of work during the great depression of the 1930's, how he had found one job but through no fault of his own, had been fired. As a result his family went on relief. This, he claimed, was typical of his life: he would struggle to be an effective support for his family; then for no apparent reason, disaster would strike, and the new misfortune would confirm his failure. He could readily believe that the melanoma resulted from cumulative injuries sustained through the years, now another incipient tragedy.
>
> When this ex-carpenter was again interviewed about six weeks after his thumb was amputated, he was even more depressed, but did not refer to his personal inadequacies. Instead, he displayed a "double rationalization" that reassured him about the extensions and implications of his illness. In other words, he accepted the diagnosis at this time, but showed second-order denial. In referring to an impending axillary biopsy, for instance, he said that if the

nodes were "positive," this meant that all the tumor had been caught, like debris in a drainpipe. On the other hand, if the nodes turned out "negative," it signified that all the tumor had been removed at the time of the amputation. Such a rationalization enabled this patient, a chronic, self-confessed loser, to see his future in favorable terms; whatever happened he could not lose again.

Nevertheless, rationalization did not protect him from depression. After the nodes were found to be "positive," he changed from a mood of dejection to one of resentment. He displaced considerable anger onto the psychiatrist, asserting that there was nothing wrong with his "mind," and that he was no "moron." The psychiatrist was baffled by this mousy man who suddenly roared, until he discovered that only the night before, the patient's roommate, an amputee, had become delirious, tried to get out of bed, and had fallen, injuring his head. When the patient was asked about this episode, he became more enraged, denouncing the roommate as a "moron . . . crazy . . . a fool . . . abnormal." It then seemed reasonable that the patient had displaced his own fear of death, as a person as well as a provider, to a fear of insanity.

Several months later, with the generous assistance of a social worker, the patient was finally able to talk about cancer with his family, whom he had wanted to protect. He even recognized that cancer was not another sign of futility, failure, or weakness. When the psychiatrist saw him again, the patient was very cool and disdainful. But he did speak of several prominent men who had recently died of cancer, without sharing their secret with anyone until the last moment. These men had traits he admired but was never able to attain: independence, self-reliance, and courage.

The balance between denial and acceptance changes like a kaleidoscope during fatal illness; old fragments constantly rearrange themselves into new patterns. Opinions differ about how much the doctor can do deliberately to produce a favorable equilibrium. During their training, psychiatrists are often cautioned about "probing too much," lest their patient become more disturbed. As a result, when psychiatrists who deal with dying patients approach the margin between awareness and unawareness, they fluctuate between very circumspect inquiry and unwarranted reassurance. They hope against dread that somehow the patient will infer the facts and spare the doctor from being painfully explicit.

Equivocation makes more patients worse than will direct inquiries. People are usually sorry that they cannot offer more, but in an erroneous belief that they can hurt people by speaking of painful facts, mitigate their influence by tangential half-statements. Patients deny more when they are told different things, not because they have been injured by truth. Equivocation produces still further uncertainty, and this creates an excess of denial. Professionals who confuse militant denial with reassurance and support may find themselves merely with a confused patient, who denies simply because he is becoming worse and has not been helped to achieve a mitigating level of acceptance.

> *Case 17.* A 35-year-old woman who had been operated upon for a slow-growing carcinoma of the caecum consulted many doctors during the course of her illness. As a result, her insistence upon getting reassurance from everyone produced a startling variety of intermediate responses. For example, the tumor mass tended to fluctuate in size. Although it was always palpable, sometimes it could be seen by simple inspection of her abdomen. She insisted that there was no need for concern, what grows will also recede. She asked many questions about her condition, but rarely paused to hear the answers. By magnifying trivial discrepancies between what doctors told her, she quoted and misquoted one to the other, confirming her conviction that doctors really knew little or nothing. At one period, she even managed to be treated by two physicians at the same time! When she found herself losing weight, she promptly went on a weight-reduction diet.
>
> Her optimistic facade and obdurate denial continued until she was finally hospitalized in a chronic care institution. She discovered that a distant cousin was also a patient in the hospital, suffering from a neurological disease. She became angry at her cousin, with whom she had not spoken for many years, because the cousin did not accept the finality of the diagnosis. The only occasion when she briefly dropped her denial was during an examination one day. She looked up at the doctor and said, "Don't you ever give up on anyone?"

Middle knowledge, the state of uncertain certainty, is a product of equivocation at a turning-point of a fatal illness. This uncertainty may be initiated by equivocation in doctors, but as a rule, the increased denial comes about because of unequivocal signs of decline, which even professionals find it difficult to accept.

> *Case 18.* A 32-year-old mother of two developed cancer of the breast one month after her husband died of myocardial infarction. She had a violent temper, and because her husband had so often been its target, she was uncertain about the link between her rages and his death. The family realized that the patient felt somewhat responsible for her husband's death, and insisted with a curious twist of logic that she not be told of her own diagnosis. Although the physician acceded to the family's wishes at first, he decided to speak candidly about the diagnosis and outlook after metastatic lesions made her future very bleak. She was not alarmed, but, tartly, asked him why he was now telling her something she had known all along! Then she spoke more explicitly about her rages, a topic that had only been surmised before, especially as a factor in her husband's death. She was certain that he had been destroyed by "wildfire anger," and that it contributed to her own imminent death as well. Cancer and rages were both like wildfire, and no one could resist either one. She was as much a victim as a victimizer. Both were hateful, and she resented efforts to shield or to support her. The strong first-order denial that she presented during the early phases of her illness was a half-hopeful sham. With the steady deterioration of her physical status, acceptance of decline covertly replaced denial, but she continued to act as if she knew nothing about the prognosis. While the family and visitors continued to reassure her gratuitously, the patient herself got grim satisfaction from realizing that she was immune to their crude efforts to "humanize" her.

Just as the overt denial that this patient expressed concealed her personal acceptance of the fatal link between wildfire rages, myocardial infarction, and cancer, other patients may present an openness about death that hides second- or third-order denial.

Case 19. A 56-year-old woman had been widowed in her early twenties, and had brought up her three daughters with two precepts: to be self-reliant, and not to fear death. This was a heritage from her father, who had spoken much about facing death directly, and frequently visited cemeteries with his family, merely as a didactic exercise. He died in early middle-age, but there was little mourning, because in a very authentic sense, his lessons had imprinted themselves. He was alive still, and as years passed, he was spoken of with such love that for most purposes, he was still an active member of the family.

The patient and her sisters were not only unafraid of death, but throughout their lives were never sure about the margin between the substance of death and that of life. That this contributed to an uncertainty about reality was indicated by an episode following the birth of a daughter. She developed a mild post-partum psychosis in which she repeatedly turned the light switch off and on, explaining that it was only in this way that she could determine whether she was alive or dead.

From the outset, the patient accepted the diagnosis of multiple myeloma, without qualms or questions. She was prepared for such an event, although this had not prevented her from leading a thoroughly active and gregarious life, combining an executive job with mothering her daughters. As a result, there was little mitigation and displacement during the intermediate phase of illness. She did deny any trace of disappointment, however, about not surviving to old age, but then she also denied regretting that her father had died so young. Funeral arrangements were completed under her direction. She had been chairman of her class reunion, scheduled for the spring, but had prudently selected a substitute in case she could not be available. One evening, solemnly but without self-pity, she commented that she would not mind dying that night. It was neither a forecast nor a plea nor a challenge. She professed no belief in a hereafter; cemeteries were abodes for the living as well as for the dead.

The future cannot be predicted, but familiarity with death can at least dispel our fears. Nevertheless, although she showed only a realistic acceptance that might serve as a model, the psychiatrist, beset with more uncertainty than his patient, wondered if she even believed in the reality of extinction. It would be a strange turn of events, if this woman, trained to accept death, and even needing specific tactics to distinguish between birth and death, met her own demise with such serenity because of third-order denial!

Another patient, a 47-year-old man, also seemed to accept death with the most meticulous calm and cordiality. Depressed at times throughout his life, he had undergone treatments after a cancer had been discovered, but then had called a halt, and seemed to accept death as an allotment. He too had no formal religion, and it would violate his memory, were we to impose one upon him. In talking about his equanimity one day, he facetiously remarked to the psychiatrist that he guessed he was a "victim in paradise!"

We are led by our prejudices to assume that how a person dies will be determined by how he has lived, a proposition that scarcely anyone can dispute. However, if this maxim leads us to expect that only "stable personalities" will endure fatal illness without serious fluctuations of hope and despair, it is patently incorrect.

> Case 20. A 75-year-old woman had been incapacitated with psychiatric complaints throughout most of her life. When she discovered a mass in her breast one morning, she immediately telephoned her doctor, arranged for an examination, entered the hospital on the following day, and underwent a bilateral mastectomy because he found two, instead of one, tumors.
>
> The post-operative course was smooth, and for the next two months, she was symptom-free, enjoying a degree of personal freedom she had not known for years. Then, after recovering from the operation itself, she found that her psychiatric symptoms returned. Although she felt that nothing she was expected to do was worth doing, the threat of death did not impress her. She was mildly depressed, perhaps as a trace of the severe depressions that she had been afflicted with. But the fatal illness, of which she was quite aware, seemed to shelter her from any return of the pervasive feelings of guilt and worthlessness that had been her shadow.

Preterminal Responses

Towards the end of Stage II, both patient and doctor may become physically and emotionally exhausted. Some patients may insist upon signing themselves out of the hospital after a collapse of communication or an unnecessary disagreement. Other patients may quietly seek another doctor, hoping for hope, but in most instances, looking for a means of accepting the inevitable. Conscientious adherence to treatments may deteriorate and become tenacious but optionless acquiescence to any suggestion and recommendation whatsoever. Demoralization in the patient may be augmented by decreased enthusiasm in the doctor. It is not unexpected that doctors may give cues to patients when their resources are thinning out. The result may be heightened denial: the doctor may insist that his patient will survive, though facts refute. The patient, for his part, may claim that he is holding his own, despite self-evident signs of deterioration.

When a patient interrupts treatment, disobeys instructions, breaks appointments, or even changes doctors, it is not always because he is "uncooperative." Seemingly life-threatening behavior, often termed "acting-out," may be a gesture intended to protest against the dehumanizing effect of protracted treatment and too-protective management. Unless the period of established disease, the intermediate Stage II, is used to create mutual acceptance, of people as well as illness, doctors may come to believe that patients are unappreciative, while patients may, for their part, believe that their doctors are personally annoyed at them for lack of progress. Mitigation and displacement take many forms. Not the rarest form is an effort to deny what has already been acknowledged.

Patients who apparently seek a miracle cure are not necessarily suffering from delusions of rescue. Rather, they may be searching for a sustaining relationship that will not falter as the illness worsens. Patients remain loyal to their doctors when both accept the uncertain future *and* the viability of their relationship. Indeed, when the preterminal period begins, treatment of the disease recedes, and the treatment of the person becomes predominant.

STAGE III. COUNTER-CONTROL AND CESSATION

Sooner or later, patients destined to die of a fatal illness reach the terminal stage and start the *decline until death*. However, death that is inevitable and death that is imminent are not the same. There is no average patient, but only people who typify their own idiosyncrasies. In the next chapter, I describe four terminal patients who faced death in their own distinctive ways, according to the circumstances that living and dying imposed. According to the primary paradox, death is a biological event that one cannot imagine. However, terminality, the disposition to die, begins much earlier, and has its characteristic counterparts.

It is possible to cease living as a conscious and responsible person long before vital functions actually stop. In this sense, *cessation* is a psychological event marked by progressive extinction of autonomy and consciousness. Not every person who is nearing death undergoes this psychological event. Cancer patients may know that death is not remote, but they are still unsure about extinction. In contrast, some patients who have received a kidney transplant, for example, may be so inundated with medications, operations, complications, and iatrogenic diseases, or just plain sickness that the additional life they have been granted is scarcely a life at all.

When does Stage III begin? The time of death cannot be accurately predicted because we do not know the critical factors that influence every case. We sometimes hear about patients who outlive the doctors who gave them up for dead, but more often, the doctor overestimates his patient's likely survival. The "Danger List" of critically ill patients does not accurately designate the patient who is dangerously ill. About 20% of patients who die in a general hospital, Weisman and Worden (1971) found, were not on the D.L. at the time of death. More than a few cancer patients succumb while arrangements are being made to transfer them to a nursing facility for chronic care. Some patients are predilected toward death, but there are also many who anticipate new treatments or even a vacation just a few hours before death. Other patients expect the advent of death at almost any time, but survive for weeks.

The preterminal period is typified by diminished autonomy, intractable symptoms, new complications, relapses, and drastic reduction in life-space. As a rule, the patient with a fatal illness must gradually yield choice and control to others. Cessation is indicated by a transition from control to counter-control. Decency, dignity, and composure permit a dying patient to achieve this transition with minimal conflict and demoralization. While the actual timing of death is uncertain, it is characteristic for patients in the terminal stage to exchange their own control for the counter-control of others.

Even though there are no ideal patients and doctors, let us imagine an ideal prototype for Stages I, II, and III. In Stage I, the patient should seek medical attention soon after recognizing significant changes in awareness or in bodily perceptions. The doctor will alertly make a correct diagnosis.

Then, during Stage II, the patient will accept the diagnosis and cooperate in the treatment. He asks relevant questions and, in response, his physician answers accurately, compassionately, and judiciously. In this way, the patient is assured of a hopeful and constructive alliance with his doctor, but still is prepared for uncertainty. Consequently, when the patient reaches Stage III, he will have anticipated extension of the disease, and be ready to relinquish decisive controls, with full confidence and trust that his dignity as a human being will not be compromised or abused. Stage III means that a patient is helped to delegate counter-control to others. In this way, it represents a choice, not capitulation. He is prepared for a narrowed life-space as well as a shortened life-time.

This is a fictional prototype, of course, which simplifies the contribution of both patient and physician. But a fictional physician is no more spurious than an idealized physician. After all, an ideal physician never misses a diagnosis and never loses a patient. His patients are never very sick, their illnesses are self-evident, and their appreciation is boundless for what requires little skill. The patients of an ideal physician cooperate to the utmost because they will get better anyway.

In reality, when the end of a fatal illness is reached, there are no prototypes, fictional or ideal. For both patient and physician, who share a common humanity, death is preposterous and inevitable. No doctor can incessantly promise to forestall death; no patient survives endlessly. Only a mutually articulated policy which anticipates various stages in the dying process provides for an authentic perspective. Patients should be prepared, therefore, for setbacks and irreversibility. Doctors should also be prepared for grievances and unrealistic distortions of his good faith. If doctor and patient learn to tolerate their limitations and idiosyncrasies, the end will find them neither too alarmed nor very surprised. If too much has been promised, then failure is compounded with mutual reproach. The overwhelming risk in caring for a dying patient is that the doctor may impose cessation and counter-control long before it becomes necessary. The patient may rightfully resent the secondary helplessness that the doctor's despair has thrust upon him. Even under the most favorable circumstances, dying people, like living people, can bite the hand that feeds them, simply because they must be fed. At the hour of greatest need, they may reproach the doctor with a charge of abandonment because he has not had an opportunity to transfer the choices and controls that remain.

8

The Terminal Stage

The more closely we look at dying, the more individualized it becomes. As we move further away, physical deterioration, metabolic changes, anatomical lesions, and other organic changes tend to obscure the individual significance of the patient. By standing very far from the patient, we discover the generalizations that characterize the organic process of dying, but by this time, the dying person himself may have been lost.

Experienced clinicians cannot always agree about the kind of death that any patient undergoes. The physiology of dying and even the criteria for death itself are somewhat problematic. And few observers venture to diagnose the psychosocial factors in death. While we can readily claim that dying is a process that is fully as complicated as living, because it *is* a part of living, to say that people die as they have lived is from a psychological viewpoint wholly meaningless. Illness and dying encompass obligations, commitments, and relationships rooted in the past, but dying may be a transitional period that also changes contemporary perceptions and meanings. People do not necessarily die as they have lived: Some undergo distinct personality changes, even becoming more "mature" during the terminal stage. Only one point can be considered certain: Psychosocial changes are not determined by organic changes with any predictable regularity. In other words, given the same disease, patients need not follow the same psychosocial sequences. They do not die in the same way, at the same rate, of the same causes, or within the same context of circumstances.

Some patients die with comparative equanimity, with few complaints or regrets. Others are reconciled to what must be, asking only for relief, not survival. Still other people cling desperately to the vestiges of life, fearing the next-to-last moment, struggling until they lapse into oblivion. Then, as organic death looms up, communication thins out, and contact diminishes. We can only surmise that, in some sense, everyone must protest the absurdity of an existence that flings them onto earth, generates a sense of life, and, when fate gets around to it, sweeps them off again.

The vicissitudes of organic disease do not explain the distinctive ways in which terminal patients pass through the final stages. Each patient's personality and psychosocial conditions impose traits upon terminality that are distinctly his own. In this chapter I shall describe the terminal stage of life in four women patients who died of cancer. Two were middle-aged; two were older. All had been married, but otherwise differed in their personal background, social position, economic resources, values, interests, and key relationships. Were it not their common fate to die of malignant disease, they would have had little else in common, had they ever met. I might have chosen forty, instead of four patients, or I could have cited an equal number of male patients, young as well as old. Still I would not have discovered any more specific qualities that truly indicate how terminality in general takes place.

FOUR PATIENTS

The first patient was a housewife from a village in Maine. She worked for many years in a factory; at no time had she been free of money problems, and never had been able to rely on anyone without many misgivings and suspicions. The second patient was also a middle-aged housewife, but from a prosperous, predominantly Jewish suburban community near Boston. She was affluent, and had a loyal, supportive family, but she was very dependent and demanding, using threats of illness to enforce and compel compliance with her wishes. The third patient was an aged widow who lived most of her life in a large industrial city after coming to Massachusetts from Ireland as a young girl. The fourth patient was also an aged widow, but in contrast to the third woman who lived in a state-supported geriatric hospital, had education, wealth, family background, social status, and personal qualities that permitted her full access to every privilege that society offers.

Case 21. A 59-year-old mother of a grown daughter entered the hospital three months after a diagnosis of acute myelogenous leukemia. She was weak, irritable, depressed, and had a painful, infected lesion at the site of a sternal biopsy.

CONTRIBUTORY BACKGROUND
She had been reared on a not very successful farm in northern Maine. At age 21, she married and moved to a small town about 50 miles away. Then, after a marginal marriage that lasted 18 years, her husband divorced her, so that during the next 7 years, she worked in a fish-processing plant to support herself and her daughter. She then accepted a marriage proposal from a lobsterman who promised her a home and a measure of respite from factory work.

She had few illusions about people or expectations about life. Each day found her grimly determined to survive, without joy or alarm. Depending only on her self-reliance, she accepted only things that were familiar, and feared, even hated the strange or unfamiliar. These traits emerged during hospitalization by her rude, threatening, and hostile manner. She was direct, and even crude in her demands, lacking elementary social niceties. As a result, she tended to alienate the ward staff by her seemingly unappreciative, passively rebellious attitude.

PSYCHIATRIC INTERVENTION

The staff ascribed her unusual truculence to a depression, and asked the consultant for advice about management. When first interviewed, she denied being depressed, denied being annoyed, and even denied being very sick. Aside from declaring that she expected to go home after the infection cleared, she did not wish to speak either of the future or the past. When she accidentally saw her chart one day, noting the diagnosis, "Acute leukemia; infection," she was relieved, as if a more threatening condition had been averted. Then she told the psychiatrist about her father, who had died of cancer many years before.

The consultant chose not to inquire further about the cancer. Instead, he urged her to talk about raising her daughter, because he inferred that this had been the patient's major achievement. She responded rather freely, spoke about her pride in being self-sufficient, and then about her resentment in being so incapacitated. She blamed the doctors for causing the infection, but also chided herself for leaving her house in a mess when illness required that she travel several hundred miles to Boston for treatment. During the next few sessions she stopped blaming the doctors, however, and began to be angry at her own body for letting her down.

Because she placed high value upon order, neatness, and self-reliance, the doctor ventured to talk about the uncertain future, with its unfamiliar events. When, for example, she complained about the stubborn infection, he gently suggested that while treatment would make her more comfortable, it could not really cure her illness. Her response was direct, but not hostile. Initially, she denied worry about death, but then blurted out, characteristically, "So if I have to croak, I'll croak!"

As if she realized that the doctor wanted to share the experience of dying with her, she disclosed more about herself as days went by. She confided, for example, that her family seemed to visit her less often. In spite of the realistic distances, she felt they were reluctant to see her. She wept for the first time. About one week later, the doctor met with the patient and her husband, talked about the illness, the outlook, and the intervening problems of fatal disease. At the conclusion, he said that now they knew as much as he did. The couple embraced quietly, and together, wept.

Visitors came during the next week, both because of her birthday, and perhaps because death was imminent. Even her ex-husband and his wife joined with her daughter, son-in-law, and husband for a seemingly congenial reunion. On the day after her birthday, she was more alert and responsive than she had been for several weeks. Her hair was combed, she even wore make-up, and for unexplained reasons, held a Rosary. She called the doctor's attention to a painting of a bridge that had hung on the wall since her admission. Her comment was that she wondered what was on the other side of that bridge, which was hidden. The doctor responded by again praising her courage, adding that she was in the process of crossing a kind of bridge. The Rosary, he assumed, was a token of her reflection on what was ahead. Her only answer was silence.

During the few remaining days, she was less and less accessible, but at one point, surprised the staff by asking when she could go home. At first this seemed to be another effort to deny her plight, or a sign of middle knowledge, but the question was really intended to test the staff's candor, not to solicit false hopes. She refused blood transfusions, afterward, stating that she was prepared for death. Her initial sense of being victimized yielded to a more accepting, serene acquiescence.

Two days later, she reported that just as she was dropping off to sleep, she felt surrounded by pretty blue flowers, like the wild asters that abound in Maine in the summer. Still surrounded by this kind of sentimental aura, she told the doctor that a little girl about 12, blonde and dressed in white, had stood at the foot of the bed, saying, "Now I want to cross over and help you." Aside from these reveries and hallucinations, the patient drowsed away her remaining hours. The doctor had little to do or say, except to be present until death took over.

Case 22. About one year after developing severe back pain, a 57-year-old mother of two was found to have multiple myeloma. Although she usually consulted doctors immediately for almost any complaint, she had postponed examination. She somewhat jokingly asked her physician, when admitted to the hospital, what results were shown by the blood tests. He replied, cautiously, that the blood was "50% all right." She immediately became agitated, wept uncontrollably, belabored him as if he had insulted her, and demanded a retraction. Knowing how demanding and accusatory she could be, the family also wanted him to revise his statement, and assure her that everything was 100% all right, not just 50%. The physician acceded, largely because she was rapidly becoming more agitated and depressed. Thereafter, until her death two years later, neither the family nor her doctor mentioned cancer, death, or incurable illness. Her questions were always met with blanket denials, reassurances, and optimistic fabrications.

CONTRIBUTORY BACKGROUND

Her mother had died in middle-age of unknown causes. Afterward, the patient became afraid to leave the house, especially at night. For many years she held conversations with her mother's picture which she kept on her dressing table. She also revealed that just after turning the bedroom lights out at night, she would feel dizzy, apprehensive, and had a vague compulsion to think of something unspecified, but dreadful.

She settled into a comfortable and conventional domesticity after an early marriage. She seldom ventured far from home, had few responsibilities, and spent her life in visiting and being visited by friends and family. After the birth of her son, she developed fear of harm befalling him as a result of some lapse in her care. If she went walking with him, she was afraid of falling or of being struck by an automobile, without warning. When her daughter was born several years later, she also felt apprehensive. As the children grew up, she instilled a deep sense of guilt, dependence, and insecurity in them, demanding and receiving total acquiescence to her wishes and impending symptoms. She objected to the son's marriage, even though his bride satisfied every standard she set. In contrast to her belief that the son was disloyal, she construed her daughter's dependence as a sign of devotion.

PSYCHIATRIC INTERVENTION

Although her physician withdrew his statement about the blood, the patient continued to cry incessantly, and slept poorly, spoke constantly about death, and reproached her family for allowing this tragedy to occur. Finally, after much persuasion, she agreed to speak with a psychiatrist who had treated her son many years before.

In the few sessions she had with the doctor, the patient was alternately grief-stricken and aggrieved. While she was pleased about the dismay that her illness had caused in her family, she was agonized by fantasies that her husband would remarry soon after her death. Anger and denial swept through her simultaneously, as she spoke. She could not believe that she might really have a fatal illness, yet she was angry that such a fate had befallen her. Everyone sought to reassure her, but she would thrust clothes and jewelry at them, declaring, "Here, take them! I want to see how you'll look, after I'm gone!"

Afflicted as she was, she had little inclination to control her behavior or to understand her anguish. She berated her son with accusations that she hoped he was satisfied, now that she was ill. Her principle was that good children stay close to their mother; those who do not, must pay a penalty. She was also angry at her dead mother, and put the picture away, saying that her mother had also failed her. She refused to see her own daughter, fearing that by some uncanny contagion, she could transmit the same illness to her.

Self-suffering and self-praise occupied most of the psychiatric interviews. She was capable of unqualified denial when reminded of topics she had just spoken about, and she easily reversed herself in any opinion she expressed. In short, it was impossible really to engage her in responsive discussion. Although her sister usually brought her to appointments, one month after her first interview she abruptly terminated, saying that her husband was far too busy to drive her. In the months that followed, she politely but firmly refused to see the doctor again.

SUBSEQUENT COURSE

The patient continued to demand that everyone mourn and share her misfortune, even though she berated the family for weeping. Even when she finally became bedridden and needed round-the-clock nursing, nothing was mentioned about the illness itself. The family did not deviate from its resolve not to speak of death or of fatal illness. Reassurances were given over and over, to the point of ridicule and stubbornness.

There was no relenting in the mutual denial and negation, but as the terminal stage approached, she seemed to turn more towards her son, and refused once again to see or speak with her daughter. In healthy days, she had disparaged her son's children as being ugly and stupid; now, however, she directed these epithets at her daughter. As counter-control threatened, and her incapacity became greater, she made little bargains with herself. If she could, for example, sit up without becoming nauseated, this was a "good" sign. If she went to the toilet unassisted, this, too, was a sign of improvement.

Nevertheless, just a few days before death, she pleaded with her son to help her die. Even at this penultimate moment, he could not transgress the pact that the family had made. Although he was choking with grief and unspoken thoughts, he still said that there was no danger of death. She then fell silent, but continued to gaze at him reproachfully. The barrier of silence was never breached again. Once again, he obeyed his mother's demands that he always protect her, lest she get sick.

Case 23. At age 66, a married housewife, mother of a daughter, was operated upon successfully for carcinoma of the large intestine. For the next nine years, she continued with her usual way of life until she developed a right hemiparesis. Although her husband and a widowed sister looked after her, accumulation of disabilities and dementia finally made it imperative that she be admitted to a chronic care institution. When admitted to the hospital, she seemed confused, incontinent, and was, of course, partially paralyzed.

CONTRIBUTORY BACKGROUND

The patient had been a schoolteacher for many years until her marriage at age 39. Her parents died in Ireland, and of her nine siblings, most of whom also immigrated to the U.S.A., only three kept contact with her. Her only child, a daughter, was born when the patient was 45 years old. Church and home seemed to describe her life within the small community. She had few interests, and in social situations was shy and seclusive, always fearing that she might say the wrong thing. With a few close friends, she was warm and generous, but otherwise, kept to herself. After the stroke, one year before hospital admission, she was exceedingly depressed and did not respond even to the overtures of friends.

Although she was in the hospital for seven years before her death, very little was known about her. Nursing notes were meager and perfunctory. The only evidence of any interest in her as an individual came from an occasional psychiatric consultation. She rarely spoke without first being addressed, and if she ever referred to her own feelings, the staff did not recall it. Most of the seven years were spent sitting by her bed or in the solarium, along with other aged and disabled women. She did not participate in activities, and showed little interest when her daughter and grandchildren visited. Except for a few illnesses, and the psychiatric consultations, she made no demands, and, in effect, became an invisible as well as a silent member of the patient population, someone that interns might refer to as "just another senile."

PRETERMINAL PERIOD

It was only after the patient died that information for the purposes of a psychological autopsy was obtained. Many details were lacking, of course, and can never be learned. But it was discovered that three years after her admission to the hospital, her husband died, without any record of her response. Five months later, she became very confused and noisy. She told a psychiatric consultant that her "father" had died about "five days ago," that he had been in his 50's, and that she was "about 40." She gave an incorrect date and did not identify the hospital by name. However, in checking the erroneous date, the doctor found that it was the day on which her husband had died!

Three years after this brief episode, the patient was presented to a psychiatric conference as a case of senile depression. She amazed the group by brightly and appropriately answering all questions, but still gave her age as 42. She still could not name the hospital. One month before her final illness, progressive cardiac decompensation, the patient told a nurse that she wanted to die and was looking for her father. In the last week of her life, she refused all treatments, medication, and food, pulling out intravenous needles and gastric tubes. The staff conceded that, in contrast to her passive acquiescence and confusion during most of her hospitalization, the patient seemed explicitly determined to die.

No autopsy was performed, but it would have been difficult to determine a true cause of death. There was nothing to indicate why death was apparently more desirable at that moment than at any earlier time in her hospitalization.

Case 24. Four years prior to hospital admission, a 72-year-old widow, mother of two sons, underwent a radical mastectomy for carcinoma of the breast. Regional nodes were not positive, but she still was given intensive radiotherapy to the affected area. Two years later, because of persistent pain and edema in her arm, the humerus was biopsied, and she was discovered to have fibrosarcoma. Symptomatic treatment did not help, and amputation of the arm was necessary. Six months after the amputation, her painful phantom limb sensations spread from the right to the left shoulder and arm. She required large amounts of narcotics, but despite the best of care, advice, and treatment by a legion of prominent consultants, the patient became more depressed.

CONTRIBUTORY BACKGROUND

Her husband had been a distinguished engineer who traveled widely in the course of his work. She usually accompanied him, and had many lasting friendships with people throughout the world. In addition to raising two sons and sponsoring worthy causes, she wrote poetry and short stories, as well as enjoying the privileges of affluence and culture.

Several years before she entered the hospital, the patient visited a city where she and her husband had once lived. While walking about, she suddenly developed feelings of unreality and depersonalization, followed by a resurgence of grief for her dead husband. She then started writing his biography, as much for her own self-treatment as to document his life. With the onset of the carcinoma, however, her writing ceased, but in the few pain-free intervals that followed, she prepared a brief account of her own girlhood for her grandchildren. She continued to be depressed; the combination of loneliness, pain, and invalidism made it necessary to employ a nurse-companion. Shortly before the hospital admission, the nurse-companion had to be discharged because of alcoholism. Hospitalization, therefore, seemed better than living alone, and just might result in pain relief.

PSYCHIATRIC INTERVENTION

She had not consulted a psychiatrist in the past, even though she had been seriously depressed at times. Her articulate, cordial manner of expressing herself, combined with an easy, sophisticated humor, created a guise of good health. The psychiatrist had to remind himself that this lady had, in fact, two malignancies, the carcinoma of the breast and the fibrosarcoma, as well as metastases, extreme pain, phantom limb sensations, high narcotic requirements, and a potentially serious depression. She had a knack for responding as she imagined people expected, then was disappointed when they failed to infer her true feelings. Her many consultants had widely disparate opinions, therefore, about her personality, illness, and complaints. As a result, the physicians who believed she had minimal pain tended to encourage more denial, while those who accepted the reality of extreme pain tended to prescribe larger doses of drugs. The patient was able to dissemble convincingly, while simultaneously insisting that something more effective be done.

Regardless of the differences of opinion among her doctors, it became obvious that the only treatment was whatever could palliate pain. Nevertheless, she maximized differences, then felt betrayed and even more depressed. Perhaps because they were not directly caught up in controversies about medication versus surgery, the psychiatrist and the hospital chaplain became her most trusted friends.

TERMINAL PERIOD

The patient became even more despondent when she could no longer hold a pen to write. Her keen sense of humor was gone, pain was unabated, and her helplessness was extreme. She slept briefly, only to awaken for more medication. When a neurosurgeon recommended a palliative brain operation, she openly prayed for death. Nevertheless, because her denial was strong and her loneliness profound, she continued to speak as if death were only one of several possibilities, not a certainty. She described places and people she would again visit after leaving the hospital, but it was apparent that this middle knowledge presaged death. She instigated a quarrel with the psychiatrist and sent him away several weeks before the neurosurgical operation was carried out. When he returned, she denied there had been an altercation, and even chided him for neglecting her.

As the decline continued, she expected death. "I have lost many loved ones," she said, "But I never saw anyone die. I don't know how to die." She deeply appreciated that her oldest son chose to stay at her side during the final days. She dreamed of being in a resort hotel where she and her husband had vacationed, but on the wall of the hotel room was a picture of Notre Dame Cathedral. This reminded her that her husband had died alone and unattended in Paris. When she awakened, she asked for a calendar of saints so that she could choose a good day to die. Thereafter, she seemed to dwell upon her impending death, complaining only that God, for His own good reasons, had let her linger so long. Truly, after so much travail, she was facing death with a strong sense of dignity, choice, and comportment, traits that had distinguished her life.

Death did not arrive at that time, because several days later another neurosurgical procedure was attempted. She moaned that this was not living, and certainly it was not death. Afterward, she regained consciousness enough to pray for respite and to talk with her friends and family. Then she finally succumbed.

SECONDARY SUFFERING AND ITS CONTROL

The primary purpose of survival is to be free of pain *and* to survive. In practical terms, this means that pain is the primary source of suffering in terminal illness, and there can be no effective psychological management until pain can be controlled (Saunders, 1963, 1965). We should distinguish between the primary suffering that comes from an afflicted organ and the secondary suffering that represents the demoralizing significance of total distress. Each of the four patients I have described died in distinctive ways. This was partially attributable to the kinds of people they were, but also in part to the circumstances in which death occurred. We cannot be sure about just how to manage dying patients well, because there are so many complicating factors. Any plan of management should, of course, use the talents of both the "technicians," who use surgical skill to provide relief, and the "humanists," who offer patients an opportunity to reconcile themselves to the inevitable, and, if preferred, not to die alone (Reed, 1968). Needless to say, if possible, patients should be able to choose or to refuse further procedures.

The following guidelines may help to alert bystanders, survivors, and clinicians to the most salient problems in reaching an acceptable death:

1. *Awareness and acceptance.* Denial is almost impossible to maintain, as Case 22 showed. Even when everyone combines to stretch denial wider than reality itself, somehow inner perceptions force themselves upon the most reluctant patient. Awareness of the future is a prerequisite for ultimate acceptance. Without it, there is only deception, regardless of the silence that is often mistaken for serenity. Awareness, however, need not concentrate upon death. There should be no grim litany, incessantly repeated. But when physicians and families rationalize their own reluctance to tell patients what they already know, it is because they have given up and have lost hope for themselves. Hope has a way of outlasting the facts of illness, just the way that in hypochondriasis, hope is feeble, but still resists the encouragement that reassurances are intended to provide. Open awareness assures continuity; candor opens the door to confidence, not to defeat.

Awareness and acceptance are the psychological counterparts of biological accommodation. Together, they lead to a gentle freedom.

2. *Readiness to relinquish.* Terminal patients often arrive at a conflict-less decision to relinquish life *after* primary pain and secondary suffering have been relieved. This aspect of the terminal phase is not the same as desperately wishing to die as a way out of unremitting anguish. Readiness to relinquish means that the patient is prepared to hand over decisions to the counter-control of people in whom he has confidence. To merit this confidence, however, survivors must be able to tolerate the descent until death, and even to share some of the agonal distress (Norton, 1963).

3. *Absolution from suffering.* I have used the term, "absolution," instead of "abolition," deliberately, but I do not intend to convey any religious meaning, or philosophical implication that there is merit in suffering. Short of almost total obliteration of consciousness, *abolition* of pain and suffering is probably not possible in terminal illness. However, control of pain and suffering is not only possible, but necessary.

Euthanasia is a unilateral decision of survivors who wish to obliterate their own anguish in the presence of another person's secondary suffering. While the controversy about euthanasia cannot be elaborated here, I caution against two kinds of untimely deaths: the *premature* and the *postmature* death. The premature death may be a kind of "enlightened execution," a frightening concept, at best. The postmature is one that is out of phase with the patient's wishes and expectations. Case 24 was prepared to die several days before actual cessation. So-called "heroic" procedures that postpone cessation for a few hours or days without adding significant survival may impose additional suffering.

Absolution from suffering means, therefore, that so far as possible, a dying person is to be exempted from purely technical procedures that pointlessly sustain his life. Throughout the terminal phase, the patient is consulted about the level of consciousness he wishes to maintain, and he is to be simultaneously reaffirmed as a person whose thoughts and preferences matter. Not to do this is a form of premature death. Often enough, ample medication is given only near the end when it might be more desirable to encourage verbal interchange and mutual awareness with those closest to the patient. Only a few people are truly willing to die at the same moment they are able to die. The processes of dying travel by several different routes and may not terminate together. Nevertheless, it is a desirable objective, and patients can be absolved from misguided efforts to interfere with this inner timetable.

4. *Death rehearsal.* Some patients initiate discussion about the appropriate time, place, and circumstances in which death is most acceptable. It is not unusual to find that people have already arranged their funeral, what they will wear, who will be invited, and so forth. These considerations are, in fact, no more gruesome than to plan a will or to decide about the method of interment. A "good death" seems to require some degree of rehearsal and revision for both the patient and his responsible survivors. No one, or very few people, die in isolation, without having some impact upon others. The psychosocial drama of dying is not limited to but one player. The circumstances surrounding death should allow for a strategic resolution of residual problems and, in so far as possible, elective rehearsal of grief and of postmortem events. There is evidence, for example, that patients who show pronounced premortem clarity tend to have a harmonious exitus, possibly because they have had a last-minute chance

to review the immediate future. This is in contrast to patients who feel fated to be discarded as burdensome objects. The atmosphere of alienation abrogates their clarity or choice in the waning moments. Rehearsals of death should not be misconstrued: It means that the terminal events and probable reactions should be anticipated and openly considered, not literally enacted. The bereavement process may be facilitated by an early discussion with and among the potential survivors.

9

Death from Terminal Old Age

CULTURAL ATTITUDES

Of everyone who must face death, it is often the aged, those who live longest, who have the most difficulty in finding serene and secure circumstances in which to complete life. Not only must they endure an accumulation of physical illnesses; but they usually contend with economic, social, and emotional problems that are inherent in extended survival itself. Old age is not an illness, nor is it an incurable disease. Nevertheless, the penalties and restrictions imposed by outliving one's contemporaries mean that advanced old age often does take on the characteristics of a relentless and fatal illness.

If society at large insists upon thinking that old age is almost synonymous with invalidism, dependence, and infirmity, we should not be surprised that aged people themselves feel they are the victims of a pervasive malady which has been brought on simply by not dying sooner. Senescence—

the aging process—differs from senility. Yet physicians and laymen alike too often believe them to be identical. They marvel at and patronize the aged person who is alert, active, autonomous, and who still has a contribution to make. To some people, senescence is a fatal illness which, like death itself, must be warded off with denial and platitudes.

Chater 7, *Death from a Fatal Illness*, described three psychosocial stages: (a) denial and postponement, (b) mitigation and displacement, and (c) counter-control and cessation. Terminal old age seems to follow a similar sequence of stages, although the aging process takes longer than a fatal illness does to run its course. Each stage has its typical denials and acceptances, which do not always synchronize with organic changes. Denial and acceptance start with first-order repudiation of getting older, pass through second-order denial of the extensions of aging, to third-order denial of irreversible decline, to impaired autonomy, yielding control to counter-control, and then, at last, to cessation.

Because senescence goes on for many years, psychosocial changes may be so inconspicuous and attenuated that we may recognize the inherent "mortality" of aging only when physical complications and economic dislocations are unmistakable. But the problems of advanced old age are not limited to medical and economic issues. Alterations in perception, performance, communication, symbolic forms, and values also have been going on for a long time. Nevertheless, eventually, depletion, isolation, obsolescence, and illness are suddenly discovered, as though they were serious illnesses that could not have been anticipated.

In today's youth-centered culture, staying young has become an end in itself. Middle-age is denied, postponed, concealed, and displaced as though it were the prelude of a great tragedy. As a result, old age is denied until infirmities of nature and rules of society overtake self-deception. This technological age often considers skillful and judicious men obsolete before they are prepared to retire. The unskilled worker may become a surplus commodity in early middle-age, but even a trained man may become technologically and administratively unskilled and, therefore, surplus because his job has been supplanted by newer instruments, occupations, and methods. Wisdom and experience are lauded, but really only in rather sentimental articles about the unspecified benefits of growing old. The old does not give way to the new; the new inevitably thrusts the old aside. Only in tribal life and early traditions do the very old have a distinct place in society (Simmons, 1945). Even then, it may just be a myth constructed over another myth.

It is an empty folly to deny the inexorable process of aging, nor is this chapter primarily concerned with resolving occupational and economic hazards in old age. This book deals with the psychological problems of death, and this chapter mainly with death in that phase of advanced old age called *terminal* old age. These are problems that transcend obsolescence, retirement, and other vital issues of society itself.

Few people can reach the arbitrary point that determines the cultural institution we call old age, without undergoing serious diminution of self-esteem. There are, of course, some people who are old while still in their twenties. These "young fogies" simply carry along the conservative values and thoughts of the past into a reactionary present. They do not realize that the innovations of the past become the principles of the present and the encumbrances of the future. There are other people who remain productive, spontaneous, and even creative until very advanced age, sometimes despite physical limitation (Butler, 1967). Every age and decade have their stereotypes, but the psychological and physical complications of old age need no more be the hallmark of aging itself than juvenile delinquency is typical of adolescence. People with an active mental life that is based upon training and interests which have equipped them for continuing enthusiasm are less likely to show the perceptual disorganization and cognitive rigidity once thought to be representative of old age (Kastenbaum, 1964). Although obsolescence is inevitable, these people are able to prolong a dignified presence in the world. Maslow (1967) has used the idea of "metamotivations" to explain how people who are fulfilled in their basic needs can preserve zest and productivity as independent qualities, even though they do not seek further recognition or economic rewards. These are some of the significant factors that preshape terminal old age, in addition to social worth, economic solvency, and flexible, age-appropriate values.

SOCIAL WORTH AND MEDICAL INTEREST

Nursing homes, extended care facilities, and health statistics attest all too clearly that when people get older, they have more need for the services of physicians, nurses, and other health professionals. Let us consider candidly the preterminal period of advanced old age, especially as it affects the doctor-patient relationship. Sooner or later, an older patient reaches a time when his physician starts to minimize complaints and ascribe ailments he cannot diagnose or cure to the inexorable forces of "old age." However, old age is *not* a medical diagnosis, but a new social role that the doctor imposes upon his patient. Because this new role requires that the older patient accept symptoms as the only alternative to health, survival itself is no longer spontaneous, but rather the earliest intimation of terminality.

A counsel of resignation is not really counsel at all. It is a plea, if not a demand, that the aged person accept his foreshortened future and not ask his physician to intercede. Indeed, the doctor himself seems to feel that old age is an incurable, chronic disease that one should be willing to tolerate. At this point, the helplessness of the physician becomes a cue for the hopelessness of his patient.

However, the problems of aging, even to a physician, are not wholly medical. The threat implied by old age, with its obligatory intimations of mortality, is not decided only by physical infirmity, but substantially determined by the *social worth* of the patient. We are not being cynical when we observe that the aged V.I.P. often discovers that his social distinction itself makes his ailments worth treating! This does not merely mean that the rich can buy more, but it does mean that social esteem on any basis can help prevent derogatory judgments about old age itself. Hollingshead and Redlich (1958) found that poorer, less educated patients are more apt to be diagnosed "schizophrenic" than are those of higher status. Among the aged, the diagnosis of "cerebral arteriosclerosis" is more final when a patient of lower social worth demonstrates confusion than it is for one with personal resources, substantial background, and relevant relationships. True, patients with higher social worth are not immune to cerebral arteriosclerosis, but it often does not become the central issue. They are thought to have more therapeutic potential, and professionals tend to provide services that another patient of equal age and equal cerebral damage, but who is a nobody, might not receive.

Case 25. An 80-year-old economist was admitted to the hospital after a third coronary thrombosis. He survived, but was so depressed that psychiatric consultation was requested.

The psychiatrist learned that the patient was deeply concerned that, by dying, he would abandon his aged wife. The couple had been married for many years, but had no children nor close relatives. They had outlived their friends and, since his retirement more than a decade before, lived on a small pension. They were able to maintain a dignified appearance by asking for very little, reducing their needs to essentials, and by living in a deteriorated section of the city.

During his talks with the psychiatrist, the patient disclosed much about his earlier life that had not been elicited on previous admissions. He had come from aristocratic lineage in Germany, and his wife was descended from equally prominent New England forebears. The patient had been awarded the Iron Cross for valor in the First World War, but his land and wealth were confiscated long before World War II. He did not talk about wartime experiences to gain sympathy, but only to illustrate that he had faced death many times before, had seen better men than he die at a much earlier age, and was not now afraid of death. However, he worried lest his wife not be able to survive, were he to die and leave her bereft and alone. They had lived through the religious, social, and political upheavals in Europe and, at a comparatively advanced middle-age, had started anew in the United States. He had to work in a bank, because university appointments in economics were not available. Their single wish was to have a reasonably secure and healthy old age until, as it must, death would come.

Investigation revealed that, at the time of his two previous admissions, none of this information had emerged. After hospitalization, he had been given only routine instructions, most of his questions were unanswered, and he was permitted to return to his slum residence. Therefore, he continued to climb stairs and to travel a considerable distance to the outpatient clinic for follow-up visits. Social service referral had been perfunctory and its results insignificant.

As a result of the psychiatrist's interest and intervention during the present admission, the entire staff became concerned about providing more care. The social worker arranged for convalescent hospitalization and found appropriate housing. Financial assistance was offered judiciously and staff physicians, learning that this was not an ordinary old man, stopped by to chat, to explain the treatment, and to suggest other measures for comfort. Although the specific medical treatment probably did not differ from one hospitalization to the other, the ensuing therapeutic relationship generated an atmosphere of hope and interest. The intangible concern of nurses and doctors could not be measured, of course, but it seemed to promote more comprehensive treatment, mostly because the patient had become *visible* and *important*.

Even when their diagnoses are the same, patients who are expected to do well often do better than those with a poor prognosis. We do not know why, but sometimes the outcome is due to some kind of self-fulfilling prophecy or therapeutic enthusiasm. Very old patients seldom are either diagnostic or therapeutic challenges, so the optimism and interest that is generated depends upon some external but adequate personal compensation to the professionals. This need not, of course, be monetary, but whatever it is, the social visibility of the patient is enhanced. In medicine, a "good case" is either one that is hard to diagnose or presents another challenge. In any event, some patients are visible, while others are simply statistics. We may preach about the equal worth of every patient, but if this were true, no patient would ever be called a "crock." In fact, most of these tend to comprise the very old or those with whom there is no open channel of communication. Anonymity and disinterest are consistent with conscientious medical treatment, but when recovery is doubtful, diminished social worth determines the structure of death (Sudnow, 1967).

Because hospitals reflect the prejudices and assessments of society, very little is expected of the aged, and very little may be offered them. If everyone seems to agree that terminal old age is only the penultimate pause before cessation, then the death of a very old person in a hospital is an almost casual, everyday event. Seniority in itself implies exhausted potential for social worth and, therefore, for viability itself.

The death of a child is always a tragedy. It is unforgettable and futile, because so much of a child's worth depends upon unrealized potential and its capacity to evoke tenderness. In contrast, the death of the very aged fits into an acceptable order of nature and we find reasons to explain why it is right and proper for an old patient to die when he does. "It is just as well." "He was about ready to die anyway." "I don't think he wanted to live." "He never took care of himself." "He couldn't have lived much longer." The terminally aged may be as helpless as a child, but they seldom arouse tenderness. Younger people are sometimes relieved when the aged die, because death appears so bleak and relentless that they cannot forgive anyone who is standing on its threshold. The very old patient, who is also impoverished and exhausted, invisible and isolated, is relegated to a kind of social class, similar to the way old people in some primitive tribes are considered to be dead as soon as death seems imminent.

PREPARATION FOR DEATH

Few people, even the very aged, willingly accept death without a quiver of regret or remorse, or without remnants of the struggle to survive. Counter-control is inevitable, but despite many indications of shortened time-perspective, fear of death, denial of mortality, and will to live are apt to have different meanings for the very old than for the young.

We live in the present, but are burdened with the mental equipment of the past. Technology may be up-to-date, but the standards, values, and purposes with which we live may be out-of-date. For the very old, many of their values, perceptions, beliefs, and symbols were wrought in a world that is so different from the world of the young that communication is like reaching back into the century before. Cognition and intellect may be faulty in old age, but, even were they not, communication across the years into the viable world of the present may be almost impossible to achieve. Obsolescence may have a biological substrate that accentuates minor organic defects and social alienation, but chronological gaps are always there. Intrapersonal isolation may create an even larger split between life and death.

What kinds of preparation for death are feasible in terminal old age? Death *ought* to be most acceptable when there is agreement about one's self-expectations and those of the community in which we live. Such consensus is seldom agreeable, however, because appropriate death requires a measure of choice and congeniality that is not just an end-product of illness or an index of social disregard.

Preparation for death is as idiosyncratic as the texture of life itself. If, however, the response to incipient death combines medical prognosis, social esteem, and personal identity, and can be strengthened by death rehearsals and by strategies that overcome denial, then death can hold less terror, principally because we have learned respect for our own existence. As already pointed out, the dread of death entails many of the inherent fears of life. Death signifies a reversal and repudiation of the values and aims we sought in life; we fear needless death, premature death, unnecessary suffering or any kind of suffering, unwarranted pain, and loneliness, failure, or death before our potential is exhausted. Death and disease, disease and degradation, and degradation and damnation are often thought of as equivalents. Our pretensions notwithstanding, we have not yet secularized existence, so we tend to see death as a punishment or penalty, and involuntarily think of dying people as lost souls, as though death were the final censure.

TERMINAL OLD AGE AND THE
PSYCHOLOGICAL AUTOPSY

Preparation for death is certainly not the same as adaptation for a healthy old age. When, however, old people who are facing death are given mental health nostrums, without heeding their individual requirements, we betray an ignorance and disrespect for existence that belies our pretensions. What is of preemptory importance is to study systematically how aged people do, in fact, enter the terminal phase. One method of such a study is the psychological autopsy.

When Shneidman and his colleagues introduced the "psychological autopsy" as a way to study suicide victims, they gave additional impetus to the psychosocial investigation of death (Shneidman, 1969). The standard, or somatic, autopsy is an indispensible tool of scientific medicine. Without postmortem study, medicine would still be in its empirical, prerational, or magical era. However, a regular autopsy tells only what a patient died with, not what he died from, and certainly not what he lived for. Even when the autopsy discloses the cause of death, it does not reveal the total context in which a person died.

The psychological autopsy is a systematic effort to determine the context of death, and to reconstruct the preterminal and terminal events and conditions surrounding the death. In general, it is intended to supplement the regular autopsy by understanding the social and emotional forces that contributed to the patient's terminal illness. Several years ago, Weisman and Kastenbaum (1968) developed a version of the psychological autopsy for geriatric patients. They investigated the medical, social, and psychiatric precursors of terminal old age, which included the retrospective reasons for hospitalization, the salient hospital events, the intervening crises and illnesses, and the final descent into death.

Despite efforts to glean relevant information from various sources, they discovered that psychosocial data are exceedingly elusive, and far more difficult to obtain than observations about organic disease. An aged person may live for years in a chronic hospital, yet his interests, activities, and ordinary habits are not recorded, and possibly not even observed. However, when he becomes ill, as older people must, there is no lack of competent attention. Again and again, however, the status of psychosocial information is apparently so low that it almost never is taken into account in the diagnosis or in planning a therapeutic program.

The higher the professional rank of staff members, the less familiar they are with patients as people. Nurses usually pay close attention to their charges during physical illnesses of any magnitude, but they, too, know little about the life circumstances and reigning psychosocial problems that patients face after recovery. Consequently, psychological assessment usually depends upon very informal observations and impromptu interventions by lower echelon staff members. These spontaneous interventions, naturally enough, are never reported or recorded.

In reconstructing earlier events, investigators usually find their path strewn with tantalizing uncertainties. The more distant events are even less definite, and to fill in the gaps, speculation and conjecture must be called upon. To put it simply, psychosocial data and observations are just not taken seriously by people tending the patient. There is a wide split between how the staff thinks the patient ought to have died, and the way the patient did, in fact, die. The split itself should be studied, because it reveals how preconceptions distort and disguise observations. This may help to improve methods of diagnosis and treatment, because, just as in the regular autopsy, we must ask where errors occurred and in what way they might have been prevented.

PSYCHOSOCIAL DIAGNOSIS: RENUNCIATION, CAPITULATION, NULLIFICATION, RESOLUTION

The psychological autopsy helps us to learn more about terminal events, but it cannot reach backward and answer questions that should have been asked while the patient was still alive. It is obvious by this time that we should always emphasize the distinction between the disease as an impersonal entity and the "patient-hood" of the person who is sick. The illnesses that afflict the aged are not always official diseases. What was he like as a person? Did he expect or want to die? How incapacitated, confused, or lonely was he? Might we have done things differently? These are simple questions that could be answered easily—were people only willing to ask and to listen. In order to assess a patient from the psychosocial viewpoint, we should ask questions about social worth, visibility as a person, medical interest, and the social expectations held by the family, staff, or ward personnel.

Preparation for death and the predisposition to die may take place concurrently and are often parts of the same process. A preterminal patient may not know how to express his inner perceptions of impending extinction, and we, the professionals, may not be able to reach these intrapersonal dimensions of experience. When we make a judgment about survival, the evidence may, therefore, be entirely superficial or peripheral. A truly comprehensive psychosocial diagnosis takes intrapersonal attitudes into account. These are actual changes in perceptions and in communication, and are not limited to transient mood changes or periods of confusion (Lieberman, 1961).

What does a "psychosocial diagnosis" really mean? We can expect, for example, very aged people who are thrust into a strange environment to become confused, depressed, hopeless, or invisible, as they retreat from "institutional shock" (Aldrich & Mendkoff, 1963). If communication and self-esteem deteriorate further, these people may become merely compliant and neutral organisms, of little significance to themselves or anyone else. By means of psychosocial assessment and diagnosis, however, we seek to define the pervading circumstances and contexts that contribute to deterioration and invisibility. When someone is told to "conform, don't complain," there are few alternatives except pointless rebellion or annihilation through becoming as inconspicuous as possible.

Psychosocial factors range from wide differences in ethnic, educational, cultural, and economic status to the immediate conditions in which the very aged must reside (Lowenthal, 1963). These circumstances include other people, possessions, pursuits—any form of contact or communication, both physical and psychological. Diagnostic terms themselves may be revealing; aged patients may be said to "misbehave"—an epithet that has been carried over from first to second childhood. They may be unruly, untidy, refuse to eat, or have petulant outbursts, and these responses may presage impending death.

The list of terminal responses is endless. In general, when cessation impinges upon their limited orbit, many very aged and preterminal patients follow one of four feasible courses. These courses may be termed *renunciation*, *capitulation*, *nullification*, and *resolution*, and each may typify terminality.

Renunciation carries a trace of choice and control, even in the face of external pressures to yield passively. Capitulation is like true renunciation in the way that falling downstairs resembles walking downstairs. Renunciation preserves dignity and individuality; capitulation demands surrender, the silent, sullen surrender that may be masked as acceptance. Anyone who has observed long rows of senile patients sitting docilely in state institutions can imagine how different these people might have been when first admitted. Standardized environments transform individuality into uniformity. Protest is usually misdirected or futile. The very aged and the chronically ill often pay a terrible price for insolvency. For this variety of terminality, there is only one style of survival, or none at all. Preparation for death is psychosocial stupor.

Nullification is a strategic obliteration of personality simply to facilitate the advent of death. The aged may not only capitulate but may define themselves as administrative nullities. It is said that perceptual rigidity is characteristic of the very old. Not only do some aged patients insist upon fixed structures in their environments and find it difficult to accept even minor changes in daily routine, but they may become just one or another fixed category in their existence. Many senile patients are disoriented for time, place, and situation, but they have also almost forgotten their names, as well. If an examiner persists in questioning them about mundane matters, such as dates, these patients may suddenly flare up in anger, as though they recognize their deficiency and do not want to be reminded of something that no longer matters. Far more serious than simple disorientation for environmental cues is loss of personal identity; this is nullification and is a sign of approaching demise.

The concept of nullification, denial of the person by the person himself, may be difficult to comprehend unless we realize that some people spend years in an institution without even knowing or caring about the name of the patient in the next bed or chair. Furthermore, the patient himself is seldom called by his correct name or title. This is nullification of social viability, or another step toward death. Patients may have memory loss, but may not want to be reminded of it; they cannot forget what they were.

Resolution is a course of behavior that enables a person to relinquish choice and control while preserving social worth, productivity, and self-esteem. It has more inherent activity and resolve than mere renunciation.

Resolution does not mean that an aged person believes the clock will be turned backward and old alternatives will be regained. Resolution means only that a strategic equilibrium has been achieved between control and counter-control, without forfeiting individuality. Death is still an ever-present reality, but not an overwhelming enormity. Acceptance is not acquiescence, and acceptance without denial can be fostered with the cooperation of significant other people. Under favorable circumstances, the reduced autonomy that follows along with the aging process relieves people of responsibility and blame for earlier problems.

We need not dwell further on the inherent hardships of insolvent old age, nor mitigate the pain by allusions to "growing old gracefully"—whatever that means. Although many aged people do seem to mellow, even more tend to deteriorate without resolution. Productivity is an indication that a person still has a sense of the future, and that his hope and self-esteem are linked realistically, not in vain self-deception. Sachs (1951) depicted the way a creative artist can transform anxiety about death into tangible art forms, and that this kind of expression produces triumph over conflict. I do not suggest that the very aged can revive long-dormant creative potential, or that this proclivity is even accessible to very many people. But anxiety about death can surely be recognized, it is wholly possible to articulate the relevant past with the immediate present and imminent future. Reminiscence, review, and true self-regard may simulate some qualities of the creative act, so that the minutiae of everyday existence need not obscure the acceptance and resolution of death. Anna Freud commented that altruistic surrender may be a protection against fear of death. Usually, it is the most deteriorated victim of terminal old age who fears death most, largely because the regressive process itself recalls secondary fears, premonitions, and dreads.

THE PRETERMINAL PERIOD

The preterminal period is that distal part of Stage III just before gathering physical and psychosocial forces coalesce into actual cessation. We can examine the signs of the preterminal period from two viewpoints, as part of the life-cycle, and as a clinical incident prior to death.

We can all agree that longevity is never long enough, and that mere survival without significance is scarcely worth the effort. It is also not enough simply to postulate that senescence and incipient death belong to a life-long developmental process, with cultural sequences and phase-specific problems.

Several developmental theories of aging have been promulgated in recent years. Erikson's theory of epigenetic development is, of course, the best known, but he has done no more than sketch in the tasks facing the aged (1966). Cumming and Henry, Havighurst, and many others have suggested still other types of conflict and crisis resolution (Williams, Tibbitts, & Donahue, 1963). Kastenbaum has proposed ways that biological information about the aging process might clarify concomitant psychosocial events.

Information about very advanced old age is fragmentary and more than a little biased. We do know that longevity and senescence are significantly influenced by such factors as socioeconomic disability, recent bereavement, serious illness, retirement problems, and chronic, nonfatal disease. Recently, Brill (1969) reviewed the psychosocial tasks inherent to old age and proposed that, in order to help constructively, the worker, as well as the aged person himself, must believe in the realistic feasibility for change. This means that support and collaboration are indispensable, especially when society itself conspires to demand defeat. The aged person has many tasks and problems unique to his stage of life that could use resources and potential for significant change. These range from basic economic requirements, housing needs, and health to cognitive problems, self-perception, adjustment to modification in the human situation, and, finally, to acquiring a measure of emotional fulfillment. If these tasks can be even partially resolved, then maturational development has called upon viable capacities, not simply the left-overs.

A developmental theory of aging that noted only progressive decline would be equivalent to a pathological preterminal period. If our observations are limited to losses, infirmities, and devaluation, then, naturally, advanced old age is simply that stage of life just this side of death. But the natural consequence of a healthy life is not an obligatory superannuation, an inescapable defeat. Many investigators object to the theory that old age itself is sufficient reason for disengagement; ill health, retirement, diminished interactions, and social obsolescence may produce secondary disengagement, or, more simply, disuse atrophy of the spirit. If we knew or cared as much about senile mortality as we do about infant mortality, sources of danger might be recognized and proper treatment instituted. As it is, however, psychosocial factors that determine how and when old age becomes terminal old age belong to a segment of life that is taboo, like death itself. Thus, terminal old age becomes an institutionalized symbol of depletion, disease, defeat.

SIGNS OF INCIPIENT DEATH IN OLD AGE

A preterminal patient reveals various signals and portents of incipient death, but observers may read these signs merely as indications of momentary tensions. It is not unusual, for example, to learn that an aged patient awakened one morning and inquired about a relative he had not seen in a decade or more. A staff member forgets the query or attributes it to senility and confusion. Nevertheless, although the strange question seemingly came from nowhere and was without rationality, it may later be recalled as a premonition of incipient death.

Of course, retrospective recall is filled with omens and auguries. Many of these premonitory "signs" are very banal and scarcely to be credited as accurate foreboding of the future. Still, some preterminal statements or actions are unusual enough to be taken seriously as revelations of an inner preoccupation or perception of impending death. Just before the descent until death, some patients divest themselves of possessions, as well as of precious thoughts and memories. Whether any person succumbs while busily planning next week's activities or declares that he will not live beyond the next few days, our task still is to recognize the circumstances and personal events that produce different attitudes (Feifel, 1956).

The psychological autopsy has schooled us to reexamine clinical incidents that precede death. If we reverse the longitudinal course of terminal events and, instead, work backward from death (D) to events that occurred at D minus N days, seemingly arbitrary and adventitious occurrences may almost beg for understanding. However, before we can systematically study the clinical incidents of terminal old age, there are three prerequisites: (a) a *theory* flexible enough to encompass both developmental potential and pathological events, (b) a *perspective* that appreciates how death and dying may take place over a long period of time before actual physical decline, and (c) a *method* of diagnosis that weighs psychosocial factors as carefully as it does organic and physical changes. By fully using these prerequisites, we are then able to learn more about selective vulnerability to death at particular times and in critical settings.

"MY FELLOW-PROFESSIONALS . . . ."

In disciplines that are as old and as new as geriatrics and thanatology, you and I have to ask many old questions and prepare ourselves for many new tasks. Generally speaking, we are skilled and compassionate, but we were trained in a tradition and in fields that cannot be readily transcribed to the problems of advanced old age and of death.

We have chosen to spend much time trying to develop

guidelines and resources for care of the aged and terminally ill. It is not easy to do, both economically and emotionally, because people do not want to face the adversities of old age, and certainly want to postpone death as long as possible. And what can we tell our colleagues and the public at large, to whom we look for help? We have few incontrovertible facts. To some extent, our principles are platitudes, or else are fallacious extensions of empirical truths wrought in the tranquillity of offices and clinics. When dealing with advanced old age, we sometimes confuse social problems with personal conflicts and tend to overlook one by favoring the other. Nevertheless, we all know that adequate care is not concluded by providing better housing, by supplementing inadequate incomes with even more inadequate financial aid, nor by setting up community resources for medical diagnosis and treatment. None of these will solve the legendary problems of getting older and of being ill-equipped for survival.

Society expects us to have answers, only because society has been unwilling to ask realistic questions. It has been content to rely upon stereotypes, oversimplifications, and clichés. The social disenfranchisement of advanced old age transcends geriatrics and thanatology. It is a product of society's failures and phobias; but our job is not to bemoan the defects in our culture, nor is it just to help the very aged put up with poverty, impoverishment, and incipient death. After all, do we merely ask adolescents to adapt themselves to the "teens and twenties"? Can we really revise our sentimental images and bleak expectations of aging and death? Perhaps it is wholly unattainable, but can we improve the social worth, cultural expectations, economic solvency, and emotional commitments available to the aged? Why must old age always be thought of as the enemy? Is it not also a distinct, respectable developmental stage, with special tasks, values, innovations, and solutions?

You, too, have struggled with the very old and terminally aged. So you already know that what we find and what we do are determined in advance by the scope of our own preconceptions and unspoken hypotheses, few of which are rooted in solid ground. How would our preconceptions hold up, were we immersed in terminal old age? Perhaps we might question each other:

1. If you faced death in the near future, what would matter most?
2. If you were very old, what would your most crucial problems be? How would you go about solving them?
3. If death were inevitable, what circumstances would make it acceptable?
4. If you were very old, how might you live most effectively and with least damage to your ideals and standards?
5. What can anyone do to prepare for his own death, or for that of someone very close?
6. What conditions and events might make you feel that you were better off dead? When would you take steps to die?
7. In old age, everyone must rely upon others, even upon people like ourselves who are professionals. When this point arrives, what kind of people would you like to deal with?

I do not know the answers to these questions, except my own. I do know that to answer these questions honestly requires starkest self-examination, and that there can be no genuine consensus. As professionals, we should recognize that service to the very aged and dying needs more than good will. We need a coherent science of death, because the more we know about terminality, the more profound is our understanding of all life. Despite our tendency to dodge and deny, we can improve our methods for detecting and dealing with terminality, wherever and whenever it is found. We might even be able to help make death more acceptable and appropriate.

10

Indications of Impending Death

PSYCHOSOCIAL DEATH

Until the very recent past, the physical signs of death were clearly defined. Absent respiration, impalpable pulse, and pooling of blood were usually sufficient to confirm what the doctor already knew—the person was dead. True, sometimes the signs were uncertain, and there were stories of unexpected revival and resuscitation, even tales of premature burial. But, on the whole, organic death and the cessation of all life were largely synonymous and unambiguous.

Today, with intensive care units in most hospitals and with vastly improved techniques for organ transplantation, the criteria for determining the moment of death have become a challenging legal and clinical problem (Ayd, 1962). In the search for acceptable organ donors, it is imperative that the doctor know when a person is about to die so that his viable organs can be used for someone else, who may also be preterminal. One person, however, will be selected for resuscitation and transplantation, while the other will die and his organs survive in the body of another. This means that we are often confronted with a new clinical problem: a dying patient whose organs will be saved, while he perishes. Furthermore, many patients who were once considered moribund are now rescued with a regularity that has become almost routine. When a patient begins to die or is dead cannot be merely a legal problem: It is an essential part of treatment, and therefore of life itself.

The moment of death is a product of consensus, and is not an incontrovertible fact. Physical signs are helpful, of course; laboratory tests, such as the electroencephalogram, lend certainty. But there may still be a quiver of doubt. In general, we already know that people may die gradually, and that there are different degrees of irreversibility for different organic systems. Even patients with the same disease die in different ways, at different times. Anatomical lesions and systemic symptoms in themselves do not establish precisely the predicted survival. Feinstein (1968) has proposed a system for classifying cancer according to both structural changes and clinical symptoms, but, to my knowledge, his system has not been widely accepted. Some studies have found that cancer survival is affected by socioeconomic factors, and still other work has indicated that survival may be substantially influenced by psychosocial factors yet undetermined. Despite decades of careful study, it is surprising to discover that the average survival rate for patients with different types of neoplasms, corrected and uncorrected, is still open to clinical conjectures.

It is a clinical truism that some patients, given a poor prognosis, may yet outlive their doctors. Even patients with several serious illnesses can live on, baffling everyone who treats them. Conversely, there are patients who succumb unexpectedly a few days after their doctor has confidently pronounced them fit, or, more commonly, given them a prognosis of several months, if the diagnosis happens to be a fatal illness. The time of anticipated survival seldom is measured correctly. More often it is a function of the doctor's optimism or pessimism, neither of which is a reliable standard. Many hospitals maintain a "Danger List" to assure themselves that patients who are in danger of dying are reported to the administration and to families. For the most part, the Danger List is highly unreliable; only a minority of D.L. patients die while so listed, and there is still a substantial number of patients who die unexpectedly. We are always dealing with probabilities when predicting survival. This means that the expected survival, or time of death, can at best only be a shrewd approximation for the individual patient. Who dies faster and who dies more slowly than the expected survival?

The psychiatrist has no more precognition and clairvoyance than anyone else, perhaps even less. However, physicians should acknowledge that disease alone cannot account for the time of death. The fact of dying is a confluence of biological, social, and psychological forces, gathered together and intersecting only at a fateful moment. Consequently, we live with the uncertainty of death; not only does this mean uncertainty about any death, but also about the factors which culminate in death. Like any living process, dying always occurs within a *psychobiological medium*.

Sudnow (1967) has pointed out that most "diagnoses" are cultural conventions, with few absolute claims, and that even "diseases" are socially sanctioned. Medicine's annals are filled with examples of diseases that were once clearly defined, but then vanished into other categories. Diagnoses may be simple items of fashion, nothing more, especially when based upon scanty lesions or ephemeral agencies. The common causes of death are usually said to be natural, accidental, suicidal, and homicidal. But this classification is convenient, not accurate. It is our scientism that excludes human and personal elements and decides that only lesions matter in determining death. However, no one lives or dies in a test tube or in a laboratory cage; social and cultural influences permeate how we live and die, and with what malady we fall sick.

The concept of a "psychosocial death" arouses antipathy among laymen and scientists alike. Our cultural bent is to blame death on organic factors, even if few abnormalities can be found. Nevertheless, it is absurd not to recognize that psychological forces may alter the psychobiological medium. Not only are so-called psychosomatic illnesses very common, but the onset of various unquestionably organic diseases can be traced to such psychosocial events as bereavement, depression, despair. It is not wholly speculative to propose that patients with chronic illnesses may capitulate at some transition point or crisis, and start the descent that terminates in death.

Psychological death does not necessarily mean psychogenic death, nor must we violate scientific canons to consider the social process of dying. Cultural preconceptions decide who is thought to be sick or well. Dying is seldom done in private, even though it is a lonely business. When people become very sick and die, they also participate in special ceremonies and rituals pertaining to the passage from life to death. Some of these rituals are, of course, quite formal, but others happen so regularly that their ceremonial significance is overlooked. For example, onlookers and mourners usually voice their sentiments about the sick person, and advance different opinions about the nature of death, age, meaning of life, and so forth. Their expectations influence how the dying person feels, and their comments are apt to modify the bereavement process.

After all, people can only die or be killed. Everything else is technical and cultural superstructure. People die a little at a time, and may even be killed a little bit, in many ways, short of actual destruction. Physical death may be gradual, and part of the significant influence is determined by psychosocial changes and expectations.

It is not unusual for a dying person to imagine and even foretell his own death. Disability, dissolution, intimations of the future may flesh out general perceptions of illness. These versions of what life still holds and what death will soon exact are not prognoses, but fantasies of life that have psychosocial significance. How we anticipate the immediate future, whether "facts" are denied or not, is a psychosocial portent, not a scientific opinion.

People often prophesize death in order to gain control over someone else. This is what "curses" and "witchcraft" are about, of course, but these threats and special ceremonials are not only intended to manipulate people, but to test their fidelity. For example, an aged lady always controlled her family by developing an incipient heart attack. At these moments, she would call her sons and daughters together and exact death bed promises. Privately, she was sure that she was not in danger, even though she had moderate arteriosclerotic heart disease. However, after recovery from these histrionics, she reproached the family for reneging on their promises. The point of this example is that this lady's image of death was to force a contract upon her family, so that she could continue to exert influence upon them, should she die. She could, self-righteously, claim that it didn't matter whether she died or not, the family wouldn't live up to the pact, either! The scenes were not merely play-acting, but a rehearsal of the circumstances in which she would find it acceptable to die. Ironically, when she did die, there was no portent. She was alone, and could not replay the familiar script.

Predictions about our future are seldom clairvoyant. Usually, our visions of the future are concocted out of our mood at the moment and our wishes, fears, disappointments, and illusions. Prediction of our own death is a statement about life, not an augury about death. Some dying patients, however, knowing that their life is limited, do voice a preference about dying at a particular time. These are often significant holidays, anniversaries, or the date of a long-anticipated event, such as a child's wedding, graduation, and so forth. While occasionally the preferred date actually coincides with the actual date of death, there are more cases of disappointment than of fulfillment.

Largely, predictions of personal death are extrapolations of despair and ineffectuality. Only a few people, like Hans Zinsser (1940) in the *Autobiography of R. S.*, predict their demise scientifically. It is feasible that incipient death can reveal itself in a portent, but third-order denial, treasured until the last, may prevent patients from recognizing and translating the message.

Psychosocial factors can elicit strong portents just as effectively as organic changes. For example, some men undergo retirement depression, especially when they give up jobs without adequate preparation for the future. Emotional underemployment and social disenfranchisements are as harmful as other kinds of poverty and alienation. All of these can give rise to portents of death.

Medicine forgets that man is more than a simple organism struggling to survive. Man's humanity requires that his superstructure be significant survival, not mere survival. He must have a measure of competence and pride to complement his significance. Work or position in society sometimes provide this reward, giving a sense of fulfillment and approval. Since society has its built-in sanctions and values, the nature of this affiliation and fulfillment varies from person to person, from men to women, from age to age. Lacking these indications of significance, the alternative is what has been called *alienation*, that bleak existential plight in which one is aimless and normless. In order to feel *healthy*, we abide by standards that reward us with self-esteem as well as physical glow. In order to feel *successful*, competence is usually measured by what society deems right and proper. Success, however, is a very parochial value, confined to an industrialized, semi-open society. But there are corresponding canons of psychosocial significance in most societies, I venture, that endow physical health with its measure of self-esteem.

Psychosocial significance is an indispensable dimension of personal death, and when it is lacking, we go looking for it. The world is far too large, too frightening, too arbitrary to comprehend, unless we personalize random events and happenstances and read them according to the vocabulary of our provincial viewpoints. As a result, we tend to find meaning and fatefulness in misfortunes, transforming the accidental into the purposeful. When one man was told about having leukemia, he paused soberly, then told about deserting a girl almost at the altar, many years before. Ever since, he had expected retribution. Like a fugitive who is apprehended at last, he seemed somewhat relieved by the diagnosis.

Portents are often self-fulfilling prophecies, not just special interpretations given to arbitrary events and accidents. A man who carries a weapon because he expects trouble usually finds an occasion to use it. A child who is expected to learn slowly often becomes a slow learner. Potential school dropouts and behavior problems may be encouraged to fulfill the contradictory messages from people in authority. The good results achieved by certain psychotherapists depend, to a substantial degree, upon the enthusiasm and expectations of the therapist. Each of these people, the man with a weapon, the slow learner, the dropout, the psychotherapy patient, receives a portentous message which can also be construed as a psychosocial value.

Any method purporting to study behavior has its implicit standards and expectations. Self-determined criteria and predefined outcomes are "contaminants" of social research, but by-products of clinical practice. Hospitals are not laboratories, so it is axiomatic that the atmosphere of a hospital or sickroom can be therapeutic or anti-therapeutic. By *atmosphere*, I mean something stronger than such bland terms as "social environment," "psychosocial structures," or "context of relationships." Atmosphere keeps us alive. It is a living manifold of interactions and identities that unites sickness, people, symbols, things, rules, and behavior. Atmosphere is part of life and helps direct what we do with that life. There are anecdotes about legendary, venerable doctors who could, it is said, "smell" the presence of an exotic disease when entering a hospital ward or sickroom. These may, to be sure, be purely apocryphal, but there are many instances in which a doctor's acumen has been prodded in a particular diagnostic direction by the surrounding atmosphere of a ward, the excitement of the house staff, and the circumstances prevailing in the hospital that day.

We are the air we breathe, including that aura generated by human interchange. We suffocate or survive, according to the emotional atmosphere in which we find ourselves. A patient who is in a life-and-death crisis may also be caught in an anti-therapeutic atmosphere, in which salient facts and perceptions are avoided and distorted. Consequently, he may slant his own communications and thoughts. Then, because people surrounding him mouth platitudes and truisms, the double-edged effect may be for everyone involved to repudiate each other, while remaining physically present and officially concerned. For example, if a dying person finds himself being treated like a hopeless case or like a child who cannot understand, he may become hopeless about himself, plead that he does not understand, and be convinced that he is worthless, as well.

Glaser and Strauss (1964, 1968) pointed out how much strife and anguish can result whenever the expected trajectory of death is violated, especially if a patient lives too short a time, and "suddenly" dies, or if he outlives the expectations. One of our patients was a 40-year-old man who had suffered enormously through a long illness of his young son. At the eleventh hour, the son had an unexpected remission. For the next few months, the son was fairly well and the father comparatively happy, allowing himself to hope that the remission would be indefinite. When relapse occurred, and his son again became terminal, the father now found himself unable to grieve. He was unnaturally calm, as if it were likely that another last minute reprieve was possible. His son died, but the father then felt guilty for not mourning more openly. Even his bereavement seemed awkward and contrived; he had done it before, and could not repeat his sadness. Several months after the son's death, the father consulted a psychiatrist, complaining of symptoms resembling those his son originally complained about before the diagnosis. He also stated that it was difficult to realize, even now, that his son was dead. The remission had, in a way, not been welcome, although social requirements insisted that he be pleased with another extension of life. Then, when death and dying came a second time, he was closed off; grief had been done, but his guilt did not acknowledge the finality of death even after the boy died.

The preceding discussion concerns "psychosocial death" as it is usually presented—and usually overlooked. Inevitably, whenever we speak about psychosocial death, people are apt to be reminded of voodoo death, hexing, bone-pointing, and other exotic topics (Burrell, 1961). Although we are not likely to find these psychological deaths at first hand, psychogenic death is not indigenous to distant places and primitive cultures. In our larger cities, witchcraft is not unknown. Amulets and magical potions are openly sold. I am informed that spray cans containing magical potions are even available.

The salient question for us is not whether psychic factors alone can induce or prevent death. We must, however, recognize that even in our culture, it is possible to feel bewitched, without believing in witches, to feel cursed, simply because of pervasive, unrelenting guilt, to believe in doom, when we are afflicted by dogged misfortune. Belief in magic and other supermundane forces cannot be obliterated by a simple appeal to rationality and reason. After all, few of the beliefs we hold are based upon their scientific validity. For those reared and dying in certain societies and subcultures, the reality of sorcery and witchcraft needs no documentation. One man's absurdity is another man's belief. Moreover, to believe in curses, omens, spirits, and the malevolence of the dead is far more persuasive because of our traditions than is belief in science and proof. Of course, *we* know that sorcery is impossible, witchcraft is only a state of mind, and evil spirits are mere externalizations of fear of death—for us.

Psychosocial death is an intertwined fabric, not a causal chain. Our habit of removing psychosocial factors from our concept of disease and death has led us to think that only "organic factors" can be lethal. There are cases which indicate that psychosocial factors seem to precipitate a fateful, even fatal outcome. Naturally, these examples are anecdotal, may be circumstantial, and could mean only that coincidence can be compelling. There are false positives, but also false negatives. A patient may openly wish to die; when death does occur without known cause, the wish and the fact may be construed as an oracle, proving the force of "the will to live" by its absence. This is a false positive. But there are cases in which signs of impending death, communications about death, and preterminal events have been ignored. When salient information is disclosed during a psychological autopsy which might pertain to death at that time, we then realize that there are false negatives, too. On both sides of the question, unwarranted appeals to scientism or slanted observations needlessly prejudice our assessment of psychosocial death. One solid case, and there are many, deserves careful examination by anyone open to persuasion; statistical analysis is not always very convincing. Respectful attention to psychosocial context does not commit us to believe in psychosocial determinism.

PREMONITIONS OF DEATH

The late movie executive, Harry Cohn, had a fixed belief that he would die at age 67, according to a recent biography (Thomas, 1968). His mother and two brothers had died at that age, but few people really expected Cohn to succumb in this superstititious way. Three years before his death, he underwent an operation for a thyroid nodule. After this, he began to lose his incredible energy and became more anxious and preoccupied. Then Cohn's only remaining brother died suddenly at 67, and about the same time, Cohn lost a lucky ring. Afterward, he talked more about death, seemed to deteriorate, and was afraid of being alone. Six months before his 67th birthday, he died of an ailment resembling coronary thrombosis.

Similar stories are told about other prominent people, and probably could also be told about ordinary people, except that their arrival and departure are not reported so extensively. *Death in Venice* (Mann, 1936) is the story of a man in whom physical illness and psychological regression created a curious premonition of death. Love, death, and the idiosyncrasies of time and catastrophe run through the writings of other authors, notably Camus. *The Plague* (1948) may be considered a novel of psychosocial death in which premonitions and portents became a way of life.

Sometimes newspapers report examples of premonitions of death which are so sensational that were we to insist upon naturalistic explanations, these would be more mysterious than the events themselves. To be sure, it is reasonable to explain Cohn's death naturalistically. To die at age 67 is not uncommon, nor is fatal heart disease unusual in hard-driving Jewish executives. After a physical illness and many business reversals, depression, despondency, and preoccupation with death can be expected. Moreover, fear of being alone, identification with family members one had feuded with and feels regret about, combined with superstitions, such as losing a lucky ring, and a paranoid personality—few people would dispute the psychopathology that these events suggest. Cohn had alienated many of his former associates and friends, so it was not unexpected that he feared being alone. Nevertheless, death at age 67 was a family tradition that Cohn did follow. Was it a true positive or false?

Legend has it that Francois I, Duke of Brittany, had his brother strangled on a contrived charge of treason. On June 7, 1450, he received a document, signed by his brother, now dead, which ordered the Duke to a trial 40 days later before the judgment seat of God. Naturally, if the Duke had not died precisely 40 days later, we are sure that the tale would not have survived.

Any anecdote purporting to illustrate paranormal influences in death is always open to doubt and to naturalistic criticism. We can strain at our credulity in many cases, but still there are instances in which psychological factors cannot be easily dismissed (Von Lerchenthal, 1948; Wilson & Reece, 1964). However, instead of reiterating stories told by others, I shall report only the premonitions and precursors of death found in patients under our observation. Very reliable and qualified professionals told us about episodes that suggested a strong psychological element in deaths of people they knew, but at best, these were second-hand stories, and perhaps had been unwittingly distorted.

There are several kinds of psychosocial indicators of impending death which should be distinguished, just as psychosocial death differs from psychogenic death. *Premonition* about one's own death is a distinct portent, an inner conviction that death in the near-future is certain. This need not be a correct prediction, nor must it have the uncanny element of clairvoyance. People can be very sick, have an idea that death is not far off, and speak of it to close associates. A man who summons his lawyer before an operation that carries little risk, but revises his will, is judged to be prudent, not clairvoyant. But if he then dies unexpectedly, for whom was the death "unexpected"? Did he have a portent of his death which could be called a premonition?

Conscious anticipation of incipient death is not unusual among very sick people. It is not strange that people who are expected to die may also expect to die themselves. It is also not uncommon to find that survivors recall comments of the deceased that can be construed as premonitory. In an effort to document cases in which premonitions about death play a significant part it is important to avoid being too tendentious about marginal situations. So I shall only illustrate the problems by citing several further cases. Case 12 stands as an example of unequivocal premonition. Case 26 is an illustration of predilection to death; Case 27, a presentiment of death, and Case 28, a rather common instance of life-threatening behavior in which the fatal outcome could have been prophesized with certainty.

Predilection to Death

Case 26. A 71-year-old Greek farmer refused surgery for a chronic duodenal ulcer for about 15 years, saying that he preferred suicide to an operation, even if cure were assured. Finally, however, after sporadic medical treatment failed, he was admitted to the hospital because of intractable pain. Since surgery seemed mandatory, psychiatric evaluation was requested.

He was a pleasant, cordial man whose gray hair, firm body, and weather-beaten face showed little sign of chronic invalidism. He consented to the operation because of pain, but was not concerned about the outcome. In fact, he simply informed the psychiatrist that he would die.

The recent exacerbation of ulcer pain had followed a crop failure. This was a significant event to him, because just before, his last enemy had died. When encouraged to tell his story, the patient willingly complied, but his manner abruptly changed. He seemed to forget the time and place in speaking of the dark, fierce antagonisms that started 20 years before. His report had an immediacy, because of both his intensity and his use of the present tense: A friend unjustly accuses him of an unspecified offense and takes over the market stall where he sells farm produce. They fight, and the patient's jaw is broken. At that moment, joy goes out of living. He withdraws, never visits the market again, sends his son to take his place. Litigation goes on for months, then years. With time, humiliation, anger, and a sense of being dishonored grows. Bitterness spreads to the officials who seemingly obstruct his efforts for redress. Lawyers, judges, witnesses become his foes. Unsatisfied, he moves away from his family, and spends the following years alone.

Within the first few years, some of his opponents begin to die. Then still others die, until, at last, his assailant's name appears in the obituary column. He is now the sole survivor of a long-forgotten feud. Soon afterward, his crops are ruined by drought. This becomes an omen of death. It is time to die.

When the patient finished his strange story, his untroubled, cordial manner returned. His intensity subsided, and he turned to the interviewer for further questions. Efforts to persuade him that omens were only psychological figments were unsuccessful. After undergoing a subtotal gastrectomy, his recovery was uneventful. However, on the third post-operative day he became dyspneic, developed atrial flutter, and died within a few hours. Autopsy showed a large mural thrombus occluding the pulmonary valve.

Many people are victims of a circumscribed paranoia that still allows them to function adequately while retaining firm belief in a conspiracy. This patient lived apart from his family and could not maintain an outward semblance of occupational or family normality. He contemplated revenge upon enemies beyond all reasonable limits of anger and indignation. With each death he became more convinced that his cause was just and that his wishes were equivalent to reality. Consequently, he interpreted natural events, crop failure, ulcer exacerbation, death, as parts of a uniform system of fate. When his last enemy died, and it is not insignificant that this was also his first enemy, anger subsided, but total vindication depended upon his death. Crop failure was an augury of his contribution to the pact. He agreed to the operation, both because of the pain and because he was certain of the outcome. It was deemed proper, even appropriate for death at this point to intervene as a completion.

The foregoing summary explains nothing, nor does it account for the lethal fulfillment of the patient's ominous expectations. I have merely restated the psychiatric symptoms according to the patient's narrative. For him, however, death was a rational outcome. For the surgeon, consent to a long-delayed operation was also a rational outcome. The first "rational outcome" was that related to the conspiracy; the second, to the intractable pain. Had the patient not objected to surgery earlier, it is difficult to imagine that a psychiatric consultation would have been sought. In the hustle of a busy ward, the patient would not have insisted upon telling his story, and the strange predilection might not have emerged.

Presentiment of Death

Case 27. About five months before death, a 78-year-old retired stone mason began to complain about losing his will to live. Gradually he withdrew from ward activities and from occupational therapy, but nothing further was observed and recorded until one month prior to death, when he startled the head nurse by asking directions to a cemetery near his former home. He explained that his former employer had telephoned, asking his help in digging graves for eight people. Actually, he had received no calls, but he had outlived seven siblings.

During the month preceding death, the patient refused to leave his ward, fearing that his employer would arrive and not find him. Two days before death, he had several teeth extracted, following which he asked the head nurse if it were now time to call his sisters, about whom he had never spoken. Whether his sisters really were living could not be ascertained, but he had had no visitors for many months. Nothing more was reported for the next 48 hours. Then he was found dead, a victim of a large cerebral thrombosis.

Delusional preoccupations with death are not unusual findings in senile patients. Diminished vigor frequently accompanies general impairment of function, and this, in turn, is apt to cause withdrawal from activities and occupations that patients formerly enjoyed. It would not be surprising for a lonely man to recall his former boss, and even imagine that he was expecting to work again. That he spoke

174/On Dying and Denying

about cemeteries is also reasonable: he was a stone mason, and in a chronic care hospital, death is no stranger.

Lieberman (1966; Lieberman & Coplan, 1970) found that aged patients reveal specific psychological changes for as long as one year before death, although a study of patients awaiting heart surgery indicated that preoperative anticipation of death is not a reliable sign of poor outlook (Abram, 1965). Premonitions of death among the aged may, however, be rather more common than is generally realized. Yet other patients in the same institution are described as being active and interested in appropriate work, therapy, and recreation until the day or two before death.

A reasonable precept in these cases is that although death is in everyone's future, people are usually surprised when it comes. Nevertheless, clear and distinct presentiments of death may be found among people who expect to die near anniversary dates (Hilgard, 1969), or who cannot visualize living beyond the age at which parents died. Some older people "give up," it is said, after a family argument, or, less conspicuously, when a prized possession, symbolizing the past, is taken away or lost.

Life-Threatening Behavior

Case 28. A 36-year-old computer engineer was admitted to the intensive care unit about 3 hours after an acute myocardial infarction. Within a week, he was out of danger, but he continued to be a serious management problem. He violated rules and restrictions about smoking, demanded extra food, and refused to stay in bed. Outwardly, he was boisterous and unconcerned, denying any difficulty. At times, however, his mantle of bravado dropped; he almost clung to the doctor, asking for reassurance that all would be well *without* changing his habits or way of life. The psychiatric consultant was called because the staff correctly assumed that the patient would ignore precautions and bring about a relapse.

He was reluctant to be interviewed at first, but his desire to impress the psychiatrist soon took over. The dominant theme, it was found, was an extraordinary fear of dependency and of being restrained by authoritarian decrees. As a result, he set many tasks for himself at his work which most men would find unreasonable. He worked nights as well as days, testing his stamina against insurmountable technical problems. He envied the computer for its relentless efficiency and its ability to get along without close emotional ties. He wanted, literally, to beat the machine. He had few friends, and these were casual acquaintances who called to visit only once or twice. He bragged about his show-girl dates, but there was never a hint of a deeper relationship. This, then, was his empty life filled with the self-defeating pursuit of "independence." He smoked three or four packages of cigarettes daily, was grossly overweight, and lived by himself in a small, inexpensive hotel.

As expected, he continued to work and indulge himself inordinately, rebuffing efforts to enlist cooperation in treatment. Within one month after discharge he was readmitted with another heart attack. Once again, he fought against treatment, and failed to keep appointments at the follow-up clinic. One year later, after suffering severe chest pain for ten days, he was brought to the hospital *in extremis*. Nevertheless, large amounts of sedation were required merely to keep him in bed. During the recovery period, he resumed bragging about his vigor and popularity. When asked about his plans, he declared that several members of his family were eager to have him live with them. Actually, no one had visited or asked about him. His only relatives were two aged parents who did volunteer their feeble resources. However he soon rebelled against even this degree of dependency, returned to his hotel, and failed to keep further appointments. One morning, not long after the social worker was again rebuffed, he was found dead by the chambermaid.

It may be that a dying person is like an unattended clock that simply runs down because no one winds it. If man is only a mechanism, he may stop because a part is broken or some alien thing gets into the machinery and interferes with its operation. But the concept of "psychosocial death" requires that we find more pertinent factors in death, besides that of incurable disease and drastic injury. Deterioration, devaluation, disengagement are only three psychosocial forces that diminish people before death. The variety of ways in which people die should make us mistrust sweeping hypotheses. I do not claim that so-called psychogenic death is a common clinical event. However, there is a continuum of cases in which psychological and social factors present curious alliances with organic disease. People can and do participate in their own demise, not only in unequivocal suicide, but in ways that traditional psychiatry might call "paranoid," "delusional," and "depressed." After all, the discipline called "psychosomatic medicine" consists largely of using psychological methods to investigate illnesses of unknown etiology. There is, however, no reason to limit ourselves to a specific list of illnesses. Psychosocial study of every disorder that threatens the health and well-being of man is the primary business of medicine, and does not require the justification of a pseudo-term like "psycho-somatic medicine." If we are open to this viewpoint, then we are open to finding people who anticipate their own deaths through predilections, portents, omens, presentiments, and even bring it about through life-threatening behaviors.

11

Counterparts of Death

Portents and predilections are indications of impending death, but there are other, equally authentic images of death that may not immediately be followed by cessation. Although these counterparts of death are part of the moving scene that gradually reflects incipient death, they may exist independently.

PHOBIAS ABOUT DEATH

The commonsense view about the dread of death is disarmingly simple: Death is feared because it is unknown. Francis Bacon wrote that people fear death as children fear going into the dark. But the reasons children fear the dark are far from simple, nor is the transition from fear of the dark to fear of death apparent. There are many explanations of why children dread the darkness: punishment, helplessness, exposure to fantasies, perceptual deprivation, and so forth. It is unlikely that any child, or anyone who recalls being a fearful child, would settle for a single explanation, and this, I presume, also applies to global explanations of why mankind fears death.

To fear death because it is unknown is hardly an explanation. Fears are based upon an inner idea of helplessness. Dread of death usually elicits annihilation- or alienation-anxiety, in which we have a portent of being destroyed as an individual or cut off from things and people that mean most to us.

There is nothing intrinsically frightening about the "unknown." After all, we deal with the unexpected and unknown every day. We fear the "unknown" only when we have already invested it with the mystery of death, not the other way around. Dread of death is a confluence of common fears which are projected into a universal destiny. Many of these fears represent debasements of values and aims held in high esteem during life, so that death symbolizes negativity and defeat. Pious affirmations about the good things to follow life seem to be rationalizations intended to convert disappointment and disillusion into fulfillment.

Dread of death is a universal concern which should be distinguished from specific phobias about death that are found in various psychoneuroses and in different emotional conflicts. The thought that "I might die or be killed" is less a statement of fact than an expression of a phobia which is anchored in unresolved problems.

> *Case 29.* A 38-year-old mother of two daughters had a successful operation for carcinoma of the cervix. Nevertheless, for the next three years, despite negative examinations and frequent reassurances about her health, she became more convinced that doctors had deceived her and that a recurrence of cancer, with death, was inevitable.
>
> Ten years earlier, the patient's mother died of a heart attack while the patient was in the hospital, giving birth to her first daughter. When she returned, she left her mother's room exactly as it had been, as if she were merely away for a short time and would soon

return herself. She cleaned mother's room regularly, arranged her clothes neatly, and, in all, kept the room, and with it, the image of her mother, distinctly alive.

Her father and mother separated when the patient was in her late teens. Mother worked as a practical nurse in order to support herself and her daughter, and was rigid about behavior, responsibility, and morality. As expected, the father was a beloved contrast. He drank excessively, rarely worked, except at temporary political jobs, but fascinated his daughter with tall tales about important men who were about to offer him a strategic position. Knowing how strongly her mother would object, the patient never revealed that she would steal away from convent school to visit with her father.

She also did not tell her mother about several affairs with married men, one of which ended in an abortion. There were marriage proposals, but she refused until she found a man who was willing to have her mother live with them. As a result, the marriage was wholly one of convenience; her husband worked hard, but, most important, allowed his wife and mother-in-law to run the household.

Psychotherapy was long and difficult; the patient was amiably suspicious and tenaciously hypochondriacal. Finally, however, she acknowledged, with moderate conviction, that mother was really dead and that doctors were not, in all likelihood, deceiving her about negative examinations. However, she hedged. Because in the past she had lied to her mother, to her husband, and often to her children, simply as a matter of convenience, telling herself that a lie was more plausible and more reassuring than the truth, wasn't it likely too that doctors had the same reason for fooling her? Wasn't she filled with cancer and about to die?

The biblical admonition about the wages of sin was peculiarly apt for this patient, whose sins were so much milder than the penalty she wanted to pay. She had been indoctrinated with a sense of guilt about her father, so that her illicit affection for him extended itself into affairs and an abortion. Her guilt about the abortion was strong, indeed, when she was in the hospital during her "legitimate" pregnancy. Her mother had died at this point, as if to underscore the patient's past offenses. It was not unreasonable, therefore, to deny this set of events and to maintain the mother's room just as it had been, as if she never died. Now, however, after the cancer operation, the patient was unable to believe in her actual rescue and cure; surely she had to die or be punished again. During therapy she admitted that fear of cancer and the phobia about death preceded the illness itself, and that she had frequently consulted doctors under one pretext or another, simply to be examined for latent cancer. In a sense, then, she was prepared for cancer, but not for its cure. Nevertheless, the phobia received, somewhat. But several years afterward, when she discovered that her teen-age daughter was guilty of sexual misbehavior, the phobia of imminent death returned.

ANGOR ANIMI

Many years ago, J. A. Ryle, a prominent British physician, described his own attacks of anxiety and alarm, which he termed *angor animi* (1950). Ryle was familiar with the chest pain and sense of doom that typify *angina pectoris*. Not only did he have angina, but three generations of his family had been afflicted. Consequently, when he developed recurrent attacks associated with a feeling of imminent death, he knew that they differed from ordinary angina. ". . . while resting recumbent after doing too much and thereby inducing pain or depression . . . I have dropped, at these times, into a blissful sleep. I am then suddenly wrenched back into consciousness by a surging sensation behind the sternum which seems to fill the upper thorax and to spread into the neck and head and sometimes down the arms to the fingertips. There is no pain at the time and, if there is any local discomfort other than that described, it is of a trivial kind. With this event comes the indescribable conviction, in the more pronounced attacks, that I am in fact passing out."

Other than a temporary pause in breathing, Ryle found no physical abnormalities that accompanied the attacks. He continued having angor animi until two weeks before his death. At that time he had a third coronary thrombosis. His son reported that Dr. Ryle knew that death was imminent, but did not mention the frightening symptom which had distressed him so long. Hence, we can conclude that having had many warnings of death through angor animi, when death was at last near, no further announcement, alarm, or intimation was necessary.

Ryle did not elaborate upon "doing too much and inducing pain or depression." He was unversed in psychodynamic parlance and did not differentiate angor animi from anxiety attacks. He did recognize that it was a symptom found rarely in coronary thrombosis and angina pectoris. We can supply the missing information about anxiety attacks. Patients may have both angor animi and anxiety attacks, but clearly distinguish between them. Ryle could only offer an explanation that the sense of dying is an "aura of a nervous storm having its vortex in those medullary centres upon which the act of living depends."

I have retold Ryle's experiences with angor animi, not because his account has historical value, but because his *sense of incipient death* which he called "angor animi" is nothing more than a counterpart of death, and not a "serious" sign of illness.

Fleeting imagery and transient perturbations akin to the clutch of death afflict many people from time to time. They shiver, quake, brush grim thoughts aside; they awaken from brief visions, and go to sleep not knowing if they will awaken. All these are counterparts of death, although death may be many years away and the people who have such experiences will seldom talk to doctors. We can only be sure that while fear of dying is a common occurrence, few people ever die as a result. Angor animi is not a common symptom of patients on the verge of death; indeed, the fact that death is at hand seems to dry up the sadness and dread that unhappily plague some people throughout most of their adult years. Beigler (1957) reported a small series of patients who were intensely anxious just before death, but these are exceptions, not the rule.

Case 30. During a long illness, an 85-year-old man had undergone several painful operations for carcinoma of the large intestine. His major complaint, however, was insomnia and fear of dying. He was frankly afraid of something, he could not say what. Sedation merely took the edge off his distress.

Several weeks before he died, the patient's son requested a consultant's opinion about pain medication. During the brief interview, the patient suddenly asked the doctor, "Do I have cancer?" When told that he did, the patient then said, reproachfully, "Why didn't someone tell me before now?" He seemed somewhat less troubled during the next few days, and it was surmised that the new pain medication produced better results. Besides relieving pain, however, the medication evidently improved the patient's spirits. He also ate better, slept well, and did not complain about his fear of dying. One evening, as his daughter made him comfortable just before leaving the hospital room, she said good night and told him that she would see him in the morning. The old man looked straight at her and slowly shook his head. "Are you afraid?" she asked. He answered, with gentleness, "Why, of course I'm afraid," with none of the anguish that had so disturbed him earlier. Then he went to sleep, and did not awaken.

For Ryle, incipient death was represented by a special state of alarm that aroused him from sleep. For Case 30, intractable pain, insomnia, and fear of dying were counterparts of death. These symptoms may be counterparts of conflicts known during life without necessarily foreshadowing death. Dormant conflicts can be awakened for other reasons than apprehension about death, but thoughts of death are never far removed when life's conflicts become acute. If death is to life as shadow is to substance, then as the sun descends, shadows and substances both have a claim upon reality that is unrecognized in the brightness of noon.

Case 31. A 50-year-old woman suddenly collapsed while looking at the body of her older brother who had died of a massive cerebral hemorrhage. She was rushed to the hospital, where an electrocardiogram showed signs of acute myocardial infarction. However, while waiting for transfer to the intensive care unit, she improved enough so that more conservative treatment was instituted. She was sent to a private room, and at her request, close family members were allowed to visit. Then, for the next few hours, under supervisory conditions which were difficult to fathom, she joked freely and bantered with her visitors. In the midst of the conversation, without any additional complaints, she suddenly expired.

As is so often true with indications and counterparts of death, her tragic end might have passed without further inquiry. However, three weeks earlier, her daughter had been married. One of the guests, who happened to be a psychiatrist, recalled that she approached him during the festivities, and had volunteered the opinion that she would never need a psychiatrist because she had no problems! After her death, the psychiatrist spoke to several family members and could reconstruct the events leading to her death. On the morning after the wedding, the patient's wealthy but eccentric mother arbitrarily reneged on her promise to pay the enormous expenses. Because she had counted on her mother's generosity, she and her husband were unexpectedly burdened with a huge debt, which only added to the financial load that their business already carried. As a result she became very dejected and apprehensive.

It was also discovered that three days before the wedding, she had asked for and received a "routine" physical examination. Although she had minor orthopedic problems for many years, her concern at the time of the examination was about her heart. She was so frightened that, after thorough assessment, the doctor reassured her by saying, "Whatever you die of, it won't be a heart attack!" Clearly, she was more apprehensive than she could admit about the wedding. Long experience with her mother's vindictive behavior had probably alerted her to expect just what happened. Her dejection and anxiety persisted until her brother died, also unexpectedly. Then she collapsed. But when brought to the hospital, she evidently regained a highly convincing mask of denial and dissimulation. Even without the threat of a heart attack, with which she had been concerned prior to the wedding, it would be very unlikely that, having just come from her brother's funeral, she would be laughing and joking with other members of the family. Ryle was relieved of angor animi after sustaining a serious myocardial infarction, but this patient manifested only *denial* of death fears.

DREAMS, DELIRIUM, AND HALLUCINATIONS

Dreams have always had an uncanny and persuasive appeal for mankind. It has been generally supposed that there is a select group of people to whom, for one reason or another, dreams reveal a message about the future. Dreams about death are not uncommon, but prophetic dreams about death are rare. Abraham Lincoln's dream before his assassination is one famous example.

Not unexpectedly, Jungian analysts have reported many premonitory dreams about death. Herzog (1966), for instance, correctly pointed out that modern people repress death although they know about it intellectually. ". . . they are dominated by a deep sense of the potential omnipotence of science, and regard death as a thing that really ought not to happen." In his study, *Psyche and Death*, Herzog also propounded a theory that dreams reflect the encounter with death in images which correspond to archaic and mythological images of death. Moon and Howes, also Jungians, recorded a number of dreams that were experienced by a man dying of cancer (Pelgrin, 1961).

I am not about to report prophetic dreams about death, although I am sure that, given the time and the appropriate patient, this would not be difficult. Dreams illustrate just about any theory of man and mortality that one can wish. The fact is, however, that most dying patients are simply too sick and too sedated to recall or to elaborate dreams very precisely. Nevertheless, people do tend to dream about on-going problems. Even when dreams seem surprisingly trivial in comparison with the plight of dying, it is still possible to construe the dream as a wish to "trivialize" the actual risk of death. On the other hand, there is nothing remarkable about prophetic dreams of incipient death in a patient with fatal illness. Such dreams are scarcely more than candid recognition of medical facts. Furthermore, dreams of miraculous recovery or, what amounts to almost the same thing, dreams of returning to happier days, are fairly common, but, unfortunately, not at all prophetic. Dreams of the dying are like dreams that occur under other trying conditions; they are metaphors of life in which solutions and dissolutions of problems convey themselves to consciousness, with differing degrees of alarm and reassurance to the dreamer.

Case 32. Shortly after he had a heart attack, a 48-year-old machinist imagined that he saw people dancing on the walls and ceiling of his hospital room. Several days later, he dreamed that he was polishing his dancing shoes. The patient and his wife had been avid dancers for many years. They won contests in their early years, and until the heart attack, continued to dance weekly.

While still convalescing, the patient had another heart attack. He then was forced to acknowledge that dancing was to be out of the question in the future. His next dream was that he and his wife were trapped in an automobile after an accident. To save her life, he nimbly extracted himself from the car, jumped over the cars that crushed them, and brought help. Then he awakened.

An interpretation readily suggested that while the patient could no longer dance, he could still drive an automobile, and that his agility might come in handy again.

Other dreams of people threatened with death recall earlier problems that have been solved. One middle-aged man, dying of cancer, dreamed about being unemployed, desperate, and poor during the depression of the 1930's. But he had, in fact, finally found a job, established a business that prospered later, and now, in the same way, hoped to outlive his present misfortune.

About one hour before she died, a 65-year-old woman with enormous edema of her legs dreamed she was riding horseback, a clear contradiction of her realistic plight. A 58-year-old man, suffering from weakness and profound weight loss, dreamed of wrestling with his older brother when they were boys. Then, suddenly, the brother threw the patient's shoes over the railing of a porch, which was on the third floor of an apartment where the family had lived. He watched the shoes slowly falling to the ground, as he awakened to feel a deep nostalgia that he could not elaborate upon.

One aged woman had exhausted her limited finances in a futile struggle against carcinoma of the ovary. When it became necessary to be admitted to a terminal care hospital, she denied being very sick, saying that her main trouble was constipation. She attributed constipation to having had too many, then too few enemas. On one occasion she dreamed of being in a prison. In another dream, she was evicted from the hospital, but, although destitute, she could still walk away. Near the end of her life, she had several dreams about normal defecation. Such are the simple wishes of invalidism.

A 52-year-old man with a diagnosis of leukemia denied that he was ill, but conceded that anyone, at any time, might be afraid of death. He also denied having dreams, but reported that shortly before he came to the hospital, his brother and sister-in-law had the same dream on the same night! A stranger comes to their house in the middle of the night. He knocks loudly, pounds, rings the bell insistently, trying to arouse them. Terrified, they refuse to answer the summons.

Case 33. A 72-year-old woman, dying of breast cancer, often had hallucinations about her mother, who had died about the same age. One night, shortly before her death, she dreamed about removing her wedding band. Although she wore the ring in the conventional place, on the left hand, in the dream she struggled to pull it free from the ring finger on the right hand. Finally, the ring gave way, but blood spouted from her finger.

Many years before, she had been separated from an alcoholic, abusive husband. She did not, however, seek divorce, nor associate with other men. For a long time, she hoped that he might reform. She had only meager thoughts about the dream. The psychiatrist was, therefore, free to speculate that perhaps incipient death signified the reluctant divorce which she had never sought. A wedding ring on the wrong hand might mean that her "wrong marriage" was about to be terminated anyway. By forcibly ending the marriage, as if to underscore "til death do us part," came her life's blood.

In the terminal hours and days of a fatal illness, patients are often so sick that it is difficult to differentiate waking and sleeping. Drugs, hypercalcemia, and other metabolic disturbances cloud consciousness. Delirium, dreams, and hallucinations meld indistinguishably (Alexander & Adlerstein, 1960). There is nothing characteristic about the delirium preceding death. Without an electroencephalogram, the clinician must depend upon observations and empirical criteria to separate delirium from dreaming. As a rule, patients can be readily awakened from dreaming, and will recall content. In delirium, patients are disoriented. Although they sometimes can describe hallucinations, reality testing is consistently disturbed.

Case 34. An aged woman refused palliative treatment for an advanced, inoperable carcinoma of the breast. About one year later, she was found alone in her small apartment, hiding behind a couch. When she was brought to the emergency ward for treatment, she insisted that the ulcerated lesions on her chest wall were insect bites. It was learned that she had been engaged to a man who was killed in World War I. After his death she considered becoming a nun, and though she never really entered a convent, she refused other suitors and lived with her parents until their death.

When she recovered from the delirium, a few other facts were established. In the month preceding admission, she had eaten very little, and had become even more isolated and bitter, spending most of the time imagining how her long-dead fiance died on the battlefield. She visualized his crawling to safety, hiding from the enemy, but then being bitten by insects. As he waited for death, she was sure that he thought only of her. It did not require much psychiatric ingenuity to understand that her delirium reproduced these thoughts, mirroring the last moments of life she ascribed to the man she had loved.

REVERIES, REMINISCENCES, AND REUNIONS

There is an intangible transition in dying patients from hallucinations to misperceptions of reality. One unmarried woman wanted her estranged brothers and sisters to be reconciled before she died. This wish was not to be fulfilled. However, in the few hours before death, the patient heard the doorbell ring, contrary to fact. Then, without an error, this debilitated woman called out the names of her many brothers and sisters, living as well as dead, as if they had all come to visit her on this last day of life. The hallucination filled in the gap between the sisters who were actually at her bedside and the other siblings who were not.

We can only conjecture about private thoughts and reveries. There are several collections of "last words," uttered by famous people (LeComte, 1955). In reading them, the judicious reader can be excused for finding the quotations more entertaining than informative. Most dying patients are too sick to be so articulate and witty, profound, or pious. Once in a while, however, there are patients in whom reveries, reminiscences, and reunions seem to come together.

Case 35. Shortly after her last child died, an 89-year-old widow was admitted to a chronic care hospital. She had cataracts, impaired hearing, memory loss, and general debility. No one visited, and except for routine nursing care, she was permitted to lie in bed most of the day.

Two months after admission, she attempted to get out of bed unassisted, fell, and sustained a mild concussion. As a result, she became more lethargic and confused, and even less effort was made to encourage activity. She was often noisy at night and disturbed other patients on the ward, so she was moved to a small room, where she was alone practically all the time, night and day. A psychiatric consultant talked with her one day, largely out of curiosity, not because of a specific request. She was disoriented for time and place, but recalled injuring her head because "the children were visiting and kept running around the room." She claimed to have become confused by the children, tripped, and fallen. Her diminished vision and hearing made confabulation an easy symptom to elicit, but she matched the voices and comments of her professional visitors with people from her past. Her time orientation varied. At one moment she spoke to her mother, and then responded to the same voice, that of a social worker, as if it were her daughter. When she "heard" another noise at the foot of the bed, she called out to her old dog, Spot.

Social service information disclosed that the patient was widowed while still in her thirties. She supported two daughters by managing a small vacation hotel, where families returned year after year. She and her daughters came to know several generations in the same family, and even when the children grew up and no longer visited the hotel, they remembered her with birthday and Christmas cards.

This aged lady had many organic defects. Although she was practically dead to the events of this world, she managed to populate her tiny room with hallucinations drawn from the past. She was, indeed, confused and disoriented, but the content of her mistakes were pleasant reminiscences. Not once did she refer to the death of her daughters, or to the current reality of the hospital.

Reminiscences, defective reality testing, perceptual deprivation, and simple wishes may blend into a kind of restoration for many senile patients. They often call staff doctors by the names of their minister or family doctor, and not infrequently, reverse generations by speaking to nurses as if they were their sisters or, in a few cases, mothers. As people grow older, not only for those patients designated "senile," pseudoreminiscences may multiply. After all, everyone knows about the good old days, when things were better, the world was peaceful, stomachs and pockets were full, men were upright and trustworthy, women were loyal and beautiful. The good old days usually never existed, but with a slight shift, an exchange of fact for a pleasant fiction, a rewriting of the ending, the "might have been" may quietly be transformed into "it happened." Pseudoreminiscences are forms of denial in which the story-teller enhances his own worth and self-esteem in the eyes of a needed supporter, and becomes a VIP. Reminiscences are not all memories; fantasies and historical facts need not be separated. Even a prized possession, with the passage of time, becomes a reminder of the past that never existed. Reveries and reminiscences are, of course, common in serious illnesses, only because patients can reevaluate themselves and their future in the light of the past.

> *Case 36.* A 56-year old business man recalled early ambitions to be a teacher, while recuperating from a serious heart attack. He had prospered at his work, but now wondered what the future held. His enthusiasm grew; could he teach school in the inner city? Without a college degree, he might have to finish his education, reduce his opulent standard of living, sell his business, and change his way of life. When he spoke of his ambitions to his wife, she was sympathetic but noncommittal. Not unexpectedly, he later found one reason or another for postponing any further action, and was soon back at work, no longer interested in reviving his old ambitions.

We cannot be cynical about the "death-bed" reminiscences and reveries of this man. Bittersweet memories and speculations about how life might have turned out, had another path been followed, are more common than most men admit. They, too, belong to the counterparts of incipient death to just the same degree as life itself leaves a trail of unopened doors and quiet renunciations.

Death-bed reunions are among the most sentimentalized of terminal events. Several examples have already been cited in which the reunion was with key people who were already dead. Near the moment of death, we should not expect people to make too careful a distinction between who is alive and who is dead. One aged woman said that she had imaginary conversations at night with her long-dead parents and brother. She slept better and had less anxiety, much as a child might be comforted by knowing that an adult who cared was nearby.

Hospital patients are seldom as completely alone as institutionalized patients, but it may still be important to encourage final farewells and, if necessary, reconciliations. Some people, however, may be so embarrassed by their physical plight that they refuse to see even old friends, preferring to be remembered as they once were. This is one of the advantages of candid discussion with terminal patients; their wishes about visitors may help in bringing about death with dignity. If the doctor is aware of unfinished business, he can gently suggest a telephone call to an old acquaintance, just as he might ask business associates to call upon the patient and discuss "the office." Most patients are, in fact, beyond caring, and there will be no point in reopening closed doors. Perhaps the greatest benefit derived from a death-bed reunion is that of the survivor. There can be little doubt that the final visit of the patient (Case 1) and his son, described in

Chapter 4, was significant to both of them. In general, however, death is so often considered a sordid secret that we do not realize how a healthy reunion or meeting between someone facing an inevitable outcome and a young survivor might be highly valuable. All of us need to be reminded of the reality of each generation as it passes away. We grow up with the assistance of the monuments, tools, writings, and mementoes of those who lived before us. Duration and continuity are given to us by these counterparts of death. We can also enhance the meaning of being alive by touching the edge of a life that is slipping away.

12

Death and Responsibility

Sickness and responsibility are opposite conditions of man. For that reason, the meaning of one helps to explain the meaning of the other. Responsibility and responsible behavior combines competence in practical matters with conduct sanctioned by our ego ideal. Sickness is the very opposite: perception, behavior, performance, conduct fall far short of what we have learned to expect of ourselves. We are sick only to the degree that we are not held responsible. Responsible action feels right because what we do and what is thought desirable seem to match. Sickness is riddled with despair and disparities between our capabilities and our actual performance. In contrast, responsibility grows out of an inner confidence that truth and reality are indivisible. Responsibility is to the self what truth is to reality (Weisman, 1965). The template of consciousness structures our image of the world.

SICKNESS UNTIL DEATH

Sickness means that we are less than we are—and suffer for it. Sickness forces us to compromise with responsible aims, and to contemplate the weak and bleak sides of ourselves. For the doctor, *sickness until death* means confrontation with his shortcomings. It may even generate a kind of sickness in him, because he, too, is drawn away from familiar spheres in which competence and conduct are unquestioned.

Physical illness is not the same as sickness until death. We need a brain to have a mind, but having a mind means that we transcend neural networks and are mindful of human experience as a whole. So with sickness until death: Mortality depends upon organic life, but the significance of individual life extends beyond biology to the experience of human responsibility.

The casual observer cannot imagine that anyone ever accepts death. He cannot believe that even in death some trace of responsible choice remains. We are so accustomed to the concept that sickness and responsibility are opposite states that the very idea of responsibile or appropriate death seems like a bizarre juxtaposition of unrelated notions. Consequently, when families of terminal patients are asked to help foster a dignified death, they often assume that this means deception, denial, and capitulation without choice.

Care of the dying is not a mere exercise in good will. It is a strategic effort to place ourselves at the disposal of patients, and to be a link between sickness until death and responsible behavior. Because we are professionals, we must understand the *mechanisms* of death. But if we are to help promote a responsible death, we must also fathom the *meanings* of death. Mechanisms of death refer to the ways in which we classify and schematize biological observations. Meanings of death consist of the ways in which our patient has been engrossed in human experience.

Generally speaking, to ask what death "means" is meaningless. It simply invites platitudes and dogmas. Death has only one basic meaning: cessation. From the psychological viewpoint, however, it is neither futile nor meaningless to wonder how people on the edge of extinction see the totality of their engrossment. Naturally, most dying patients are just too sick, sedated, and detached to talk about meanings, and survivors, doctors included, are too diffident to ask. Nevertheless, under favorable circumstances, it is possible to gain a deeper appreciation of what sickness until death is about.

The meaning of death is how we systematize our sufferings. How does the dying person himself look upon his suffering and his engrossment? What does having death at hand signify to him? Who are his key people? What is his view of the familiar world, now that he is very ill? What has mattered most to him during his lifetime? Does he suffer from the primary disease or from the psychosocial sickness that illness has imposed upon him? How shall we stretch the thin fabric of our personal confrontation over this final phase?

REGRESSION AND DEATH

Fear of death, dread of dying, hope, despair, denial, acceptance, predilection, appropriate death are but a few of the concepts I have described thus far. Now, however, in order to pursue our understanding of the transition from mere sickness to sickness until death, I must call upon the elusive concept of regression. It is a common enough term in psychodynamic theory, but it is hard to define, and examples of regression are not very revealing. Nevertheless, instead of using a new term, it is advisable to retain the concept, but to define it more clearly with respect to changes observed in dying patients.

In general, regression refers to stereotyped, not highly selective behavior. It implies poor control, pathological communication, and defective reality testing. Beyond these points, however, the dying or near-death patients observed during this study did not resemble regressed patients seen in mental hospitals. There was little, if anything, to indicate a "return" to earlier, less differentiated modes of behavior, except that considerable impairment was observed.

The *diagnosis* of regression is a collective judgment about different levels of experience. It requires that we know the patient very well to appreciate how much and in what direction he has changed. What was he like before becoming sick? We should also know where *we* stand with respect to the patient's current plight, because our slanted observations may distort the degree of regression. Indeed, it is uncertainty about where to stand that is part of the problem in regression. Someone with grave sickness has *no* firm place to stand and affirm himself. The problem is that he can neither stand nor stand very much in the way of novelty and initiative. He is supine and supplicant in both literal and figurative senses. Recumbence itself violates perspective and induces feelings of helplessness. For example, if we were forced to spend the rest of our life in standing on our heads, we would be certain that our legs were useless appendages, more a burden than a help, and certainly not a means of locomotion.

For many bedridden patients, the mind becomes an encumbrance. The brain is a burden encased in the head. The world is closed in. Experience, gathered over a lifetime, means less and less. They look in a mirror, and scarcely recognize the image that stares back. Other people, often those who are most important, become shadowy semblances, mere fractions of themselves. Possessions are only what is close at hand and within reach. In the daily passage from here to there, time is bunched together. The only relic of self-reliance is found in minor acts of self-care. Healthy people cannot really appreciate this predicament. For the dying person, the future is already here, and he greets each day with only residues and traces.

How shall we describe the regressive behavior that flourishes during the terminal period? There are few symptoms that are gross enough to be called "regressive," in the customary sense, unless the patient happens to have severe brain damage or is delirious. Nevertheless, regressive behavior is common, and may be recognized by contrasting it with states of health.

1. Because healthy people act carefully and selectively, regressive behavior is inappropriate and inaccurate.
2. Because healthy people have many options to choose from, regressive behavior seems rigid and stereotyped.
3. Because healthy people can face new situations without fear and confusion, regressed patients are threatened and disrupted when confronted with changes in themselves or in their world.
4. Because healthy people can readily tell the difference between inner thoughts and outer events, regressed patients show impairments of reality testing.
5. Because healthy people participate in a world of shared responses, regressed patients are withdrawn and impoverished. Communication is limited to the concrete and immediate; only what is seen, felt, and asked for is fully real.
6. Because healthy people can initiate action on their own behalf, regressed patients are largely acted upon. As a result, thoughts and feelings may be ascribed to forces in the outside world.

Regression is a clue to sickness, but in a larger sense, it is a phrasing of existence. It, too, is a polarity; regression is to its opposite, restitution, as sickness is to responsibility. If this sketch of regression seems somewhat strange, it is because psychiatrists usually confuse all regressive processes with those of psychopathology. When viewed as a condition of human existence within the psychobiological medium, however, we can identify three broad types of regression.

Biodynamic regression is the psychological and behavioral counterpart of organic disease. The sick organism responds to its own inanition, weight loss, fever, and enfeebling by-products with impaired mental function, disordered cognition, memory lapses, errors of judgment, lability of emotions, and a thousand other symptoms that betray a faltering organism.

Sociodynamic regression reduces the range and depth of human relationships. To the very sick, the world may seem too hostile and impatient, in too much hurry, to speak too fast, and people may be too slanted in their approach to everyday events. Sick people may speak nonsense, or hear absurdities. Words are grasped with difficulty, and often seem to be spoken from a great distance. Significant people lose the quality that endeared them to the patient during healthier times; they seem boring, indifferent, obtuse, and irritating. Complexities are scarcely worth bothering with, but simple episodes in the course of the day may take on highly personal meanings. Simple tasks loom up as insuperable demands, and mere passing comments become hardened grievances. When social scientists talk about sociodynamic regression, using terms like "withdrawal" and "disengagement," they lose the trenchance of this deadly predicament. Regressive simplification has a violence in its seeming calm that cannot be described with jargon and euphemisms. It is, for example, a euphemism when we say that a defeated populace is "peaceful;" so, too, a very sick patient will do whatever he can to bring about a measured equilibrium.

Psychodynamic regression is what psychiatrists usually mean by the term. But even here regression does not mean that sick people drop into preordained developmental slots and emerge with predictable behavior that professionals can recognize and call "psychotic." Dynamic theory, with few exceptions, overlooks the existential dimension in which sick people try to resolve their quandary. Who am I? How did I get here? Where am I going? For example, a regressed patient may be clearly disoriented with respect to surrounding "reality," at least as defined by consensus. However, from another viewpoint, his faulty report and erroneous orientation may be quite appropriate if we judge them according to requirements of inner equilibrium. In other words, psychopathology and symptoms may be efforts to preserve traces of responsibility, despite impaired resources.

For the most part, very sick people oscillate between regression and restitution, just as they shift between sickness and responsibility (Weisman, 1966). Each of the four terminal cancer patients, described in Chapter 8, were regressed, from the viewpoint of biodynamic, sociodynamic, and psychodynamic changes. Yet none was psychotic in any sense, and it would be difficult to find "primitive" thinking in anything they said. The dying patient usually shows signs of regression, if we look for the following:

1. Gross denial, undue projection, and excessive externalization.
2. Misuse of words, confusion about familiar concepts, fragmentation of everyday conversation, misinterpretation of the obvious.
3. Preoccupation with minutiae, disturbed communication, such as impaired ability to deal with simple abstractions, condensation and elliptical meanings, inaccurate designation and errors in common actions, and
4. Just awkward thinking.

Words and things seem to be equivalents, but habits become obstacles. Daily rituals are filled with demands and impossible effort, and even ordinary behavior acquires an element of mystery.

DEATH AND THE DOCTOR

The doctor, too, is caught up in the ebb and flow of regression and restitution during fatal illness. But because he can seek refuge behind his professional formulas and facades, we are not accustomed to considering ways in which he is affected.

What can the Doctor do about death? What is the impact upon him? I deliberately capitalize Doctor to separate the vocation from that of individual practitioners. These questions differ from familiar issues, such as the physician's traditional responsibility toward any patient, including the ones he cannot cure. The Doctor has always been endowed with magic and mystery; he is a physician and priest in our culture, especially during periods of illness when cure is unlikely, technology faulty, and treatments pointless. Ancient cultural values emerge from the sociodynamic regression. The Doctor becomes an emissary between the mysteries of medicine and the unknowns of impending death. Most modern physicians do not recognize this aspect of their profession, and would feel unnatural in situations where they are expected to be somewhat oracular and imperturbed. This is not to say that doctors are unaccustomed to making pronouncements far beyond the available facts and figures. But the well-practiced facade of the urbane physician who can talk out of both sides of his mouth at once, and be eloquent in all directions, may not be adequate in the presence of death.

The paradox of the medical profession is that the physician is both a healer and someone equally baffled by inexorable death. The Doctor, therefore, is a kind of Everyman who may come to grief at a future time, but believes that he still might have forestalled the inevitable or made it somewhat easier.

What the Doctor can do about death has two sides, professional and personal. As a professional, he tries to diagnose and treat. If he cannot, then he relieves anguish. But if this, too, fails, he continues to give of himself. Then, when death approaches, he stands by, guiding, assisting, ameliorating. This is his "professional" responsibility, which can be assigned to others, but cannot be routinely relegated. Like most ethical ideals, it can rarely be fulfilled. Lacking time as well as training, he may perform the essentials of his skill, and allow competent paraprofessionals to take over. However, the Doctor may not realize that he cannot fulfill his own ethical expectations. His traditional role at the pinnacle of the professional pyramid may create an illusion that everything is under his control, because he has not assigned his job to anyone else. What has happened is that having other obligations prevents the Doctor from following his obligations to the dying. He does not delegate; he has already forfeited.

How does the plight of fatal illness affect the Doctor? He can close his eyes, of course, or walk away, turn aside, and pretend he doesn't see. He can retreat a few steps, without actually leaving, thereby interposing an acceptable but unbridgeable distance between the patient and himself. He can also revise his participation, call upon others, and change his picture of the person who is the patient. Or he might even change his own image, donning a neutral mask for the remainder of the drama. These are but a few tactics of disengagement which typify the interaction, or lack of it, during the terminal phase.

Physical problems aside, every Doctor has tacit formulations about death that create both his problems and his resolutions. He, too, undergoes specific regressions, although he is not subject to the symptoms of the patient. The Doctor's personal regressions are products of four major *problems* and *existential positions* with respect to death: (a) probability of death, (b) obligation to die, (c) necessity of death, and (d) freedom to die.

Probability of Death

Diagnosis of fatal disease is impersonal and statistical. But as extinction approaches, terminality becomes a personal judgment. Many physicians tend to overestimate the time remaining for patients, as if wanting it so will buy an extension. Increasing probability of death means that the patient does not merely have a fatal disease, the disease has the patient squeezed in a relentless grasp. The Doctor cannot release the patient, so he, too, becomes a prisoner of probability. In all conscience, he is bound to the patient, and with fewer options, he is less the physician, more the minister, as he watches the probability of death impersonally swell until it is completely certain.

Obligation To Die

The Doctor stands by, and as the odds against survival become greater, he also witnesses changes in the psychosocial world surrounding the patient. The patient is dying; this is enough change. But the world around transforms itself in response to awareness of man's universal *obligation* to die. This problem is not a matter of impersonal statistics, but one of fatefulness, or fulfillment of an unwitting debt contracted at birth. It is as nonsensical to ask why anyone must die as it would be to ask why he was born. The only answer is that man is obliged to die; he is possessed by an illness, but this illness has only conspired with a preexisting disposition. Man is born because his mother was pregnant at the time; he dies because he has an "illness" that cannot be cured. Both explanations are redundant.

Necessity of Death

The probability of death and the obligation to die are still somewhat impersonal and social, and while they influence the Doctor's transactions with the people involved, he remains somewhat detached. Now it all becomes more personal: the necessity of death means that *my death* is guaranteed—and so is *yours*. All that is uncertain are the time, place, and staging, mere technicalities, in a way. For the patient, the blank spaces in the program are about to be filled. For others, the necessity of death or, if you choose, the allotment of mortality is not measurable until extinction is almost here. Third-order denial persists until the eleventh hour. Then we take hold of reality and death returns the clasp. Until this point, however, we maintain an attitude of *not-yet and not-now*. But third-order denial slips aside, and in the immediacy of here-and-now, the necessity of death presents itself.

Freedom To Die

We are familiar with the probability of death, because very sick people may die, instead of recovering. We are also familiar with man's obligation to die, although we prefer not to think about it. Most people grudgingly accept the dictum that if man is born, he will die—but it might not be anyone we know! The necessity to die splits our awareness, because it means *my* death and *yours*, irrefutable facts that still seem to be contested by every quiver of life we feel within. Of all these existential positions, however, the freedom to die comes as a shock. Common convention and the signs of life within tell us that death must be a catastrophe. Probability, obligation, and necessity decree that death cannot be avoided or denied. What freedom can there be in accepting extinction?

The only consolation that authentically can be offered to a person facing imminent extinction is that *freedom to die means that we have an option to die our own death*. This is a potentiality consistent with being able to live our own life. If death is mandatory, it is certainly worthwhile to have a dignified and painless death, even though it is also possible to ascend the scaffold with composure, and without freedom.

If there is no freedom without responsibility, and no responsibility without freedom, then we must select our options under the guidance of our ego ideals. When pushed to the ultimate, responsibility also includes the freedom to die, because death is an active part of living. Survival is always temporary. At the final phase of life we have only two options: to die or to be killed. This does not mean that suicide is always a responsible alternative to dying or being killed. The suicide makes a choice in order to avoid the quandary of having to choose between life and death. He appropriates death without ensuring an appropriate death. To die without the necessity of death confuses the freedom to die with its necessity. Not only is suicide a dissipation of human potential in most cases, but it is a travesty on freedom to die. Significant survival and significant death mean that we are freed from the tyranny of suffering, impoverishment, disenfranchisement, and gross incapacity.

The freedom to die is a natural result of significant survival. It can only mean that there is an inherent element of consent during the terminal period. Until counter-control and cessation arrive, then, we can be sustained with traces of personal affirmation.

REGRESSION AND RESTITUTION IN THE DOCTOR

What are the regressions that the Doctor undergoes? Although some physicians do undergo biodynamic regressions, the most conspicuous signs that a doctor feels endangered are sociodynamic and psychodynamic. He may deny grossly, externalizing his personal problems, or project blame onto others. He may become preoccupied with technical minutiae, with the rituals of practice, foregoing the patient's reality as a person. His interventions may be restricted to only one side of the entire situation, a "part for the whole" response that is characteristic of regression. As a result, he becomes worried about addiction, or, what amounts to the same thing, supplies drugs too liberally, as a substitute for consciousness and concern. This response is better known as "concrete thinking." When the Doctor talks vaguely and learnedly about abstractions, not only does he reify the intercurrent and concurrent events, but he turns "things into words," another indication of regression. The iatrogenic problem of addiction illustrates clearly how a physician's dread of suffering and denial of death may interfere with existential assessment, and produce regression in himself.

The actual risk of addiction differs from the fear of addiction. Both, however, assume that the patient will survive long enough to become addicted. In brief, worry about producing addiction in a dying patient may be a distorted version of the existential fact that someone is about to die. It is a regressive denial of the obligation or necessity of death, and may, as a result, interfere with the patient's freedom to die without pain. Fear of addiction and fear of producing addiction in terminal patients seem to have a curious ambivalence. We should also remember that doctors are particularly vulnerable to addiction, although this has largely been forgotten in the past few years when youth-oriented, poverty-spawned drug usage has so dominated our culture. Nevertheless, that physicians were the "pioneers" of contemporary drug culture, and perhaps for similar reasons, might be a hypothesis for a study. The other side of addiction-ambivalence is that although the Doctor sincerely wishes to relieve anguish and feels helpless about not doing so, he does not want to purchase survival at a death-in-life price. Consequently, he may deny death and turn his fears toward the risk of addiction, even though the expected duration of life is measured in days.

In drug habituation, life is made tolerable by regulated control of drugs. In drug addiction, a drug is necessary to life. This straightforward distinction is often forgotten because of regression in the Doctor. To fear addiction in a dying patient signifies three things: The doctor has confused addiction with habituation, he denies the fact of incipient death, and he is afraid of *killing* his patient. In short, he confuses *probability* of death (the patient may die) with its *necessity* (this patient must die). Regression in the Doctor, especially when combined with denial of the freedom to die one's own death, leads to a horrific dilemma: painful capitulation to the *obligation* to die, or promoting death-in-life survival, without meaning or responsibility.

Overestimation and underestimation of expected survival times may be wholly subjective. Therefore, these judgments can be strongly influenced by iatrogenic regressions. Naturally, we want patients to survive, but it should be survival with maximum responsibility. To withhold medication or to dispense inadequate amounts may betray the doctor's inability to accept the reality of pain and death. Indeed, it may even signify the Doctor's denial of any of the four existential positions related to death. Recently, a 22-year-old girl who was dying of chronic kidney disease requested the medication she had received at an early stage of illness. She had much pain, and although morphine was more effective than the earlier drug, she preferred the less active medication. She was completely aware of her downward course. There was no indication of heightened denial or middle knowledge.

The psychiatric consultant who had known the patient over many weeks inferred that the girl wanted a medication that reminded her of the community of care and hope she had once experienced. The staff had been attentive and supportive during the earlier stages. The patient had many visitors, and was enchanted by the miraculous possibility of a kidney transplant. However, several transplants were unsuccessful. Now, at this late stage, nothing further was planned. Inevitably, discouragement and disillusion were communicated, even though physical interaction was maintained. Of course, the patient preferred to live. But in requesting a drug that recalled a more hopeful period, she was unwittingly exercising freedom to die in her own way. Doctors, too, may undermedicate for the same reasons that this patient chose to undermedicate herself. The regression consisted of identifying the medication with the wished-for hope.

Regression may be shown in still other ways. Like anyone else who feels ineffectual at the bedside of a deteriorating patient, the Doctor may mouth insignificant words or assume an overconfident pose. The result may be called "grave triviality," in which technical verbiage, unnecessary laboratory tests, and preoccupation with academic issues become irrelevant caricatures. For all the benefit the patient derives, the Doctor might as well be a theologian discoursing about the soul and eternity.

IATROGENIC DISORDERS

Doctors sometimes reveal an unwitting revulsion about the sights, smells, and futility of caring for a "hopeless" patient. There are many "hopeless" situations because the Doctor despairs. This need not be the same as "hopeless" patients, who may, unfortunately, get that way in response to nonverbal communications. Iatrogenic distortions are often the products of too much care, not lack of skill or indifference. Erroneous judgments, mishandling, and bad medicine differ from iatrogenic distortions. In fact, the difficulties produced by the Doctor may be the product of bad faith and good conscience, not bad medicine. Here are a few examples.

Secondary gain refers to the unexpected benefit a patient gets from being ill. To some degree, when a Doctor supports a patient unrealistically, he indicates that a threatening reality can be changed into one that can be managed without distress. In doing so, he gets benefit from misleading the patient, and restitutes his own well-being, despite the grave illness.

Strategic omission is a common iatrogenic distortion. When patients turn for the worse, the frequency, scope, and length of the physician's visits also decline. Questions are seldom solicited, lest an embarrassment result. The atmosphere may be one of uneasy cordiality on both sides, a strategy which can only produce further deviation from what is desirable.

Reassurance and support are always required, but it takes a fine eye and a dogmatic mind always to draw a sharp distinction between iatrogenic distortion and the art of medicine. Not everything a Doctor does is therapeutic; he is a non-healer, too. Unsolicited, gratuitous reassurance is for the benefit of the doctor, not the patient. Moreover, inappropriate and misplaced support may fortify denial and encourage further regression.

Faulty communication may be found not only in what the Doctor says and does not say, but in his understanding of what the patient says and means. One man, for example, complained that he couldn't read after a cerebral thrombosis. "You can't?" his doctor said, "Try to read this," handing the patient a nearby newspaper with a bold headline. Of course, the man read the few words promptly. "You see, of course you can read!" the doctor responded, triumphantly. But what the patient meant the doctor had failed to understand. Since the stroke, he could read printed material but not retain the gist of what he had read. He knew what words and phrases meant, but could not connect meanings nor remember a story until its end. As he read, meanings slipped away, so that he was as impaired as though he could not read. The physician knew about aphasia, but his speciality was not that of language and its disorders. He easily slipped into a distorted viewpoint which regarded all forms of reading disability as the same. There was a clear semantic difference between the patient's "reading" and the doctor's "understanding," but there was an even greater difference in their communication. The patient was a victim of biodynamic regression; the doctor showed a corresponding degree of sociodynamic regression.

The magic healer is a role that most doctors like, despite protests to the contrary. Patients like to feel grateful, even when there is little to be grateful about. They excuse faults in a doctor because they expect to idealize him. Brusqueness is sometimes admired and condoned, as if rudeness and a no-nonsense attitude signify efficiency. An overly busy doctor is often thought to be a very capable doctor, although he may merely be avaricious. The lordly style appeals to some patients who confuse the grand manner with great confidence and skill.

The underlying assumption and danger found in iatrogenic distortions are that the Doctor taints medical issues with moral bias. What happens inside the Doctor is private, but his misconceptions and expectations are apt to create erroneous expectations within the patient. Good patients always conform to expectations, but very good patients are those who fortify the Doctor's ego ideal. For example, some physicians prefer patients who are passive and compliant, who obey instructions to the letter, and acquiesce in whatever happens. Other doctors prefer patients who try to do for themselves, without waiting to be told. The first type of physician has an ego ideal in which he takes over completely and feels needed, as good Doctors should. The second type of physician has an ego ideal in which the Doctor is resourceful, independent, and self-reliant. He encourages his patients to be the same, as good Doctors should.

Both kinds of physicians are apt to be very effective. However, when things go wrong, as, indeed, must happen in fatal illness, the first type of very good patient may be rebuked for being "too dependent," for displaying an excessive compliance that threatens the Doctor's ego ideal. The second type of very good patient, who is highly independent, may be chided when he seeks to participate in his care and to share in the ensuing fault. Such patients may blame themselves, saying, "I've been overdoing it. I shouldn't have tried to get out of bed so soon."

Doctors tend to rebuke patients when they do not "accept the limitations of disease." Or they may become annoyed when patients seem ill-motivated to get the optimum benefit from treatment, and tell patients, in effect, "It's up to you." To exaggerate a bit, the first type of patient (and physician) tends to become depressed during the late stages of illness. The second type of patient (and physician) is apt to be afflicted with guilt and unreasonable suspicion about lack of improvement.

There is a difference between the profession of physician and the existential position of being a Doctor. The practice of medicine insists that doctors be both. Terminal situations magnify this distinction, and consequently, demand a degree of flexibility and acceptance that corrects for diminishing rewards and returns in satisfaction. In sickness until death, the responsible physician needs to reduce his own regressions, and to ask for all the help he can get. A dying patient learns to yield control to others whom he has selected. Doctors, too, might learn to share their enormous burden, without forfeiting responsibility. If they can achieve this, then the impact of death itself can be modulated. This means that iatrogenic distortions are reduced, secondary suffering is alleviated, and many of the dilemmas that complicate the closing scenes can be eliminated.

13

Illusion and Incipient Death

In 1924, Freud was found to have cancer of the mouth. He underwent a long series of painful and disfiguring operations, all futile, until his death 15 years later. Nevertheless, he continued to work and to write, refusing to use even mild analgesics. His ostensible reason for doing so was that his clarity might be impaired.

During this period of cancer and the inexorable tragedy of his times, Freud became more occupied with the nonclinical applications of psychoanalysis. He wrote extensively about religion, anthropology, art, civilization, topics beyond the confines of the clinic and consultation room, as if to signify his gathering awareness of both personal death and world catastrophe. Nowhere in Freud's writing is this more apparent than in his tiny treatise on religion, *The future of an illusion* (1927). His general thesis was that man needs and seeks protection from both nature and civilization. Ultimately, however, man has only three options in his search for security and shelter. He can adhere to religious teachings, which Freud deemed illusory; he can accept religious ideas simply as mythical consolations; or he can rely upon the soft and insistent voice of reason to quiet the threat of disaster and death.

Religion, in Freud's mind, was a search for an all-protective father. However, this is a paradoxical quest; the father who will protect us is also the one from whom we need protection. The doom is ordained: at the end, man must give up his life, renouncing everything, as a slave forfeits himself to his master. Civilization makes us renounce instinct, nature threatens us with disease, so-called "natural" disasters, and, finally, death.

THE FUTURE AS AN ILLUSION

Religion is an illusory source of security, Freud wrote, because death is inevitable. Death is the epitome of every threatening force in nature and man; it is the enemy and its victory is certain. Freud argued that the rituals and reasons given for belief in divine intercession are illusions. But this is also true of other alternatives. If ultimate dissolution is absolute, then it is the *Future*, any future, which is the true illusion. The person facing death, therefore, may call upon religion or any other resource, including stupefying drugs and analgesic surgery. What death means, however, is that the future does not exist.

Religion has always found it difficult to explain why gods worth believing in permit so much misfortune, cruelty, and evil to thrive. A child, too, might be puzzled why his parents cannot protect him against pain, disappointment, and suffering, and then come to believe that his parents are responsible for his troubles. Nevertheless, to believe unflinchingly that, sometime, somewhere, somehow, evil will be punished, and good deeds, rewarded, does not seem sufficient reassurance for many people. To accept death as probable, obligatory, and necessary is scanty consolation. And because the countenance of death, as most of mankind conceives it, bears the scars and bruises of the suffering sustained during life, being free to die one's own death does not seem much of a boon.

There is always a split between the individual who faces death and his personification of death. He is unlikely to feel singled out to be the exception, yet he hesitates to conclude that he is a wholly trivial bit of biology, destined to be obliterated. Faced with extinction, he is more apt to think that we are all hapless victims of a hostile fate that takes note of us only to ignore our protestations. In order to achieve some degree of reconciliation as individuals dying our own deaths, we seek ways to make our departure less adventitious and more significant.

For people who have been demoralized by illness and misfortune, death can scarcely be worse than life. If pleasant myths and fantasies could be superimposed upon this mystery, death might even be better. People who have been favored with health throughout their life seem to take the world for granted. Like some overprivileged child who expects life to be an extended candy store, those who have known only the easy oblivion of good fortune may automatically and unquestioningly believe that what they want is synonymous with what destiny intended. Death is also viewed as a perpetuation of the *status quo*, an endless continuation of the here-and-now. Whether one believes in a future that is better, worse, or more of the same, the credo is equivalent to an indefinite postponement of death. In any form, this belief is a pure form of denial and self-deception.

This illusion of a future, that deals can be made which exempt us from dying, is linked with another illusion, that we are timeless, and have more control over the future than we do. Camus (1955) questioned how anyone can survive without appeal or reward, surrounded by absurdity. But we do live in an ambiguous present, circumscribed by distorted recollections of the past and amorphous anticipations of a future that may never come. Illusions need a sense of time unfulfilled, because time unfulfilled is its own illusion, that change is possible, and that it will be for the better.

Failure to believe in change for the better is often embedded in what clinicians call "pathology." Man tends to accept his frailties and sicknesses, because he believes in the durability of his personal consciousness. After all, consciousness means that we are not only conscious *of* something, but that we are conscious *for* something. The idea of "health" means that we believe sickness is reversible and temporary, and that we are able to act according to our own best interests *for* a future. Whatever happens, we do not question the intrinsic animal worth of being alive. When we do not believe that losses can be overcome and replaced, or that, come what may, we can be put back together again, clinicians call us "depressed." If, at times, we feel overwhelmed by a massing of evil forces or by the collective inertia of mankind, we are said to be "paranoid." If we clamor for a fulfillment of love, for realization of fantasies beyond reasonable justification and capacity, we are thought to be "hysterical," or even under some kind of spell. If we set up a strategy of practices, beliefs, and rituals to systematize the vagaries of nature and to neutralize the witchcraft in everyday life, it is only because we want to prevent the future from being worse than the present. Nevertheless, we would be "obsessional and compulsive" to do so. Thus, we pathologize our perceptions, seeking to neutralize our beliefs and to conform to a consensus.

The primary paradox is that we believe in our own survival in the midst of obligatory extinction. But the primary paradox is not wholly an illusion. While it is too much to believe that our tiny sand castle will withstand the sea, our *belief* in a future, any future, does hold our inner world together. It is neither an unmitigated illusion or a sign of pathology. It is a belief in our personal "I" and its enduring presence that determines what we judge to be real, true, or convincing on any other grounds (Weisman, 1958).

We begin and end within the limits defined by consciousness. Despite our concept of the "dynamic unconscious" and its derivatives, it becomes real only when the impact of unconscious forces registers upon personal experience. Indeed, the sharp split between the inner and outer worlds, roughly divided by our sense organs and skin, should not be regarded as a primary experience, but rather as a fact learned with great difficulty. There is a considerable difference between having a brain and having a mind. That version of reality called "the world" with such finality is in part created by the standards and predispositions that we bring to and carry away from personal experience. *Personal presence* is a given, an axiomatic "here-I-am" that means whatever is real is real for me, and whatever is real for me is real.

The crux of dying and denying is found in the reality of our personal presence. For that matter, it is this presence that personifies reality, including that of death. The reality of death transcends mere biological cessation, because we are "mindful" of death at all times, even though it is a "not-yet" which is denied, disguised, postponed, mitigated, and concealed. The reality of personal presence is such that its extinction is both a "not-yet" and a "nevermore" that happens only to someone else.

Death and time are inseparable portions of our personal presence. Clocks and calendars are convenient amulets that lull us into believing that time ends when death begins. However, the past lives only insofar as I can locate events *and* care about them within my field in the here-and-now. To be sure, we do talk about the past as well as the future, without really believing in them, just as we accept historical events without any redeeming sense of reality. That Caesar crossed the Rubicon means no more to me than that Washington crossed the Delaware, unless, for some reason, my experience of reality and time impinges upon what was real for Caesar and Washington.

The psychology of incipient death requires that we understand the double nature of time, which we call chronological and existential. The idea of unlimited chronological time, days without end, everlasting, differs from the personal reality of existential time. Chronological time *quantifies* events according to a place and space scale. Existential time *qualifies* events according to their personal significance. Chronological time is linear, while existential time stratifies events under a contemporaneous sense of reality. While we live within the continuity of consciousness, when experience intensifies, pauses, recedes, and becomes quiescent, then our sense of existential time emerges.

Chronological time is public property, but its significance depends upon how existential time impinges upon it, so that we can take possession of it. Chronological time is largely spatial and depends upon a public consensus. Existential time has no comparable units of measurement, but as we complete any action, existential time elapsed can be compared with other stretches of experience. For example, we measure how long we sleep by different readings of the clock; how well we have slept, however, is measured only by how vividly we experience the relief and resuscitation that morning brings. We are always between sections in chronological time, but we are in the midst of existential time, sharing its rise and fall.

There are many situations in which existential time is so immediate that, to speak of it at all, we must translate it into chronological time. "It seems like only yesterday," we often say, when suddenly a child becomes an adult. At other times (sic), we suspend chronology and create a consensual illusion about existential time. For example, when we watch a play, scenes and acts covering months and years take place within a few hours. We consent to suspend chronological time in favor of the total experience of the drama. If, however, we are bored or uninvolved, the action on the stage does not hang together in the midst of existential time. Until the final curtain permits an exit, our personal presence stands aside, watching only for the passage of chronological time.

Standing on top of a mountain, we can watch cars slowly moving on a road below. We are, in effect, experiencing a contemporaneous event, which the motorist, driving one of the cars, cannot experience. Simultaneously, from our position, we experience the past, present, and future of each motorist. He is obliged to go from here to there, from now to then. Our existential event is to perceive his chronological time without being a part of it, just as we do in a play, when actors undergo changes in chronological time.

It is always true that in the midst of existential time, there is no *remote* future, only the creeping edge of the present. In this respect, we are no different than the patient facing imminent or inevitable death. It is our anticipation of change that determines how far the future extends. Everything else is an illusion within the structure of chronological time.

The dying person has little besides his current reality and his existential time. If, for example, we ask him *what* he felt when he first became ill, we are asking how he feels now with respect to the *quality* of his experience then, and *not* how long or when it was that he first was ill. To the very ill, chronological time is not of primary importance. Thomas Mann depicted the contrast between existential events and chronological time in the *Magic Mountain*. When sick people state that they were "never sick until about a year ago," they are simply contrasting states of being, not dates.

The flesh of personal presence attaches itself to the skeleton of chronological time only as a matter of convenience. It is typical of fatal illness that chronology dissipates; one day becomes another, a month is only a few days, and a year may be almost irrelevant, depending upon the detachment that the patient feels. Consequently, very sick young adults, suddenly wrenched out of their life by illness, are tragically aware of the gap between what is here-and-now and the potential of chronological time, with expectations unfulfillable. Nevertheless, as they approach terminus, the agony of chronological unfulfillment tends to change, so that existential time provides a sense of completeness. It is not unusual, for instance, to find a man about to die in his early twenties who speaks about "If I had my life to live over" or "When I was young I used to . . . ."

Few patients in the throes of fatal illness ask how long they have to live, although this is a natural question asked by relatives and friends. As dying and illness go on, time is measured not by the clock, but by the intervals between visits, meals, and medication, simply because inner states of being change at these periods.

Patients who deny will usually talk about the remote future during moments of relative despair, and it is not a sign of hope. It is, rather, a response to hopelessness that creates an illusion about the future. Middle knowledge, a state of seeming forgetfulness, is characteristic of imminent death, not a sign of remission. Left to their own resources but bolstered by the continuous concern of people who survive them, dying patients will largely accept the limitations of foreshortened time, as they approach the brink that separates the *now* from the *not-yet*.

DENIAL AND INCIPIENT DEATH

Incipient death is not unlike a threat of being put to death. But as time goes toward exitus, the threat of death becomes less coercive and more subjective. It is the suffering induced by helpless survival that agonizes, not death. To survive, but with torment, to survive, but with hopelessness, to survive, but without dignity, is certainly equivalent to being killed. I have tried to convey a conviction that death is not a grim specter standing at the end of a road, like a murderer in the night. Death is a symbol for whatever bedevils people during the act of living. Given the culture of denial and dissimulation in which most of us have grown up, a society in which we are taught to be ashamed of certain realities, the meaning of death is not an idle philosophical speculation, but an extended personification of the suffering we have endured.

None of us can endure constant exposure to death. Even to believe that our own extinction is an illusion condemns us to a strategy of denial in which suffering is glossed over with professional skill. There are four major professions that mankind appoints to bring this about. Each has its special version of death and denial. The death-professions are the clergy, the military, the morticians, and the medical. None of these specialists could exist without a constant supply of deaths, but their common creed is to deny extinction so that in some form or other, endless survival is assured. For example, in the presence of incipient death, the clergy may call for a belief in an after-life. The morticians today tend to package death and to sell it as an interminable slumber. While publicly deploring death, the military also insists that to be killed for a cause is an elevating experience, and one that almost guarantees heroic stature for the soldier. The medical profession often assumes a posture of self-righteous invincibility by struggling to preserve life beyond any reasonable hope for a significant future. Medicine denies extinction by tacitly professing that any survival is better than none.

The death-professions do not recognize death as such. They fail to heed the principle that long before actual life ceases, there are many small closures and terminations. We die in our own existential time because our viability has become a burden and we have exhausted every potentiality for being something different. To die because our viability has become a liability is not like saying that we sleep because we can no longer stay awake. There are degrees and levels of viability that are essential to significant survival, even until death. We can recognize three such levels; perhaps there are more.

Primary viability is the biological condition for survival, regardless of the circumstances that must be endured simply to live. On this plane, the purpose of existence is merely to survive without pain, but with a measure of safety, fulfillment, and support. Primary viability is a moment-to-moment durability. Because there is no preemptive demand for visualizing a distant future or for contending with a world of abstract relationships, primary viability is a "given," not a problem.

Secondary viability means that we have significant choice, control, and even mastery over the events surrounding us, far beyond the mere minimum required for survival. We can act on our own behalf; we are reasonably competent within our sphere, and our goals are determined by assessment of the past and future.

Tertiary viability signifies far more than competent behavior. It endows what we do with a sense of success or regret, according to the way in which our conduct corresponds to the directives of an ego ideal.

These different degrees of viability tend to influence the kind of significant death that any person must die. It is feasible that physical deterioration can coexist with an inner belief in choice and responsibility. Biodynamic regression need not be parallel with sociodynamic or psychodynamic regressions. Incipient or imminent death can be at hand, but the person who dies in his own time may retain responsible threads of consciousness. He cannot do as he pleases or as he once could, but he may still exercise certain decisions, so that he acts with fidelity according to his ego ideal. He has no chronological future, but does he need one? Denial repudiates change, simplifies and distorts reality, and may nullify the individual. Affirmation, denial's antithesis, requires a strong sense of individual reality. Because death is the most undeniable of facts, dying and denying must be split off from each other.

The split between dying and denying during the terminal phase of life depends largely upon the people who surround the patient himself. Most dying patients do not require an illusion of the future. But the common strategies of denial insist that change is possible, and that things will be as they once were, never had been, or never will be. Denial holds time at a standstill. But death is even more compelling. To deny this fact is to risk exposing someone who is already beyond the reach of time to an empty promise of survival.

ALLOTMENT-ANXIETY AND ACCIDENT ANXIETY

We recognize, all of us, that anxiety, depression, guilt, confusion, conflict, and disillusion are sorry parts of the obligatory conditions of being alive. They become intolerable, and we become desperate, when these conditions are thought to be permanent. Thus, dying may be either an acceptable necessity or a fearful omen of something yet to come. We feel anxious in the presence of the at-hand, but we dread the not-yet.

Dying people may not show overt anxiety, but this is often because their fears have become detached from objects and things to the situation as a whole. During healthier periods, the fear of death is a semantic funnel for every other fear we can identify and dread. During the pause prior to death, however, anxiety may be represented in feelings of devaluation, endangerment, annihilation, and desertion.

Briefly, *devaluation* is seldom expressed in open self-rebuke. Patients become unusually compliant, withdrawing from everyday events and interests into a state of apathy and passivity. *Endangerment* refers to excessive preoccupation with peripheral problems, as if these were more threatening than the primary disease. An endangered person is apt to show unusual regressions, and to deny beyond reasonable expectations. *Annihilation* is a fear of disintegration, not merely of the physical self, but of the personality as a whole. Some unfortunate patients who show symptoms of devaluation, endangerment, and annihilation may be described as "victims of themselves." They are dependent, without trusting in their right to be cared for; they are without confidence in their reality testing because, in some inscrutable sense, they are already gone. *Desertion* is alienation-anxiety. It is brought about by separation from whatever supports and activities helped to generate the sense of being alive and being someone who matters. Even experienced professionals find themselves withdrawing in the presence of death, and many well-meaning people feel a natural revulsion. The sights and smells of terminal disease are just as disgusting as the thought of death is horrendous. There is often an infectiousness about the deadly atmosphere that cannot help but arouse antipathy and aversion. There are no effective sprays and deodorants for the stench of despair.

There is always hidden anxiety in whatever we do. Endangerment, devaluation, annihilation, and desertion are signs that our viability is in peril, even though physical death may not be imminent. Nevertheless, existential anxiety can be contained, if not prevented. There is a difference, for example, between the death that finds us unprepared and that which is acknowledged as one's possession. There is no better way to express this difference than to distinguish between *accident-anxiety* and *allotment-anxiety*.

Accident-anxiety is dread of an impending catastrophe, against which struggle is futile. We can no more prevent the "accident" of death than we can still the seas or mute an earthquake. Literally, the bedrock of existence melts away, and we are engulfed.

Allotment-anxiety is the fear that is part of a conscious choice. We have yielded control to another, but our forfeit preserves dignity and self-esteem. We dread, but it is *our* dread, not naked annihilation. For a person who is on the threshold of death, anxiety can either be antithetical to our previous viability, and thus, entirely accidental, or can be consistent with what is still ours. Any other outcome, through denial or heroics, may turn us all into imposters.

Our clinical study of incipient death indicates that, for most people, the normality of death is at best only grudgingly accepted. Yet, the conviction grows that consciousness, responsibility, and hope become inseparable as time evaporates. Denial at too great a price is an encumbrance. If survival for its own sake is not enough (and it isn't), or faith because we merely believe in believing is inadequate (and it is), what can any man choose for himself when reality itself is relinquished? If significant survival means that he is important enough to live, then he may find additional significance through having his own death to die.

We can all recognize a "bad" death, but find it hard to identify a "good" death. Suffering, regressions, impoverishment, hopelessness, and so forth belong to the inappropriate conditions of life and the antithetical qualities of death. Intercessions on behalf of the dying are expected to right these wrongs. The professional credentials and field of specialization are less important than is the capacity to be *there*. It is likely that professionals who are afraid of working in vain are working with a sense of vanity. To be significant does not mean that we are all-important or are required to have magical powers. If a doctor provides relief of pain, it is a substantial contribution. If he relieves pain and provides significant support, it is even more substantial. If he stands by, lending his personal presence, to conduct the patient safely from the now to the not-yet, then he does as much as possible. Secular intercessions espouse neither creed nor philosophy, other than the plain truths that the dying need allies and that the future is an illusion.

The practical significance of mortality depends upon how we come to terms with incipient death and existential anxiety. Accident-anxiety is part of being alive; we can be killed at any moment, or can fall victim to a fatal disease. Allotment-anxiety means that our death is also part of being alive, and is within reach, although we do not reach out for it.

Despite our cultural indoctrination, death is not the essence of corruption and negativity. Human values seem to be enhanced when we become aware that death always surrounds us, like the shadow that illuminates the substance. The pervasive dread in dying seems not only to be the extinction of consciousness, but the fear that the death we die will not be our own. This is the singular distinction between death as a property of life and being put to death.

In their cyclic alternation time and reality space out the passing of days and nights. Ultimately, of course, time disappears, reality diminishes, and then turmoil is left behind. For the dying person, there is resolution, relief, silence, then nothing at all. When it is finally acknowledged that the future is an illusion, it no longer matters. Yet, significant survival and dignified death provide an orderly direction to the exit. Clearly and compassionately, we find ourselves acting according to an inner mandate. The practical significance of mortality is that, denial and dread notwithstanding, it is completely within human potentiality to greet death ruefully, but without regret. The true vision of existence, denuded of everything else, as it must be when death is at hand, is contained in a preemptive demand, "Here I am, but what am I?" In a curious way, this is both a question and an answer.

Bibliography

GENERAL REFERENCES

Brim, O., Freeman, H., Levine, S., & Scotch, N. *The dying patient*. New York: Russell Sage Foundation, 1970.

Choron, J. *Death and western thought*. New York: Collier Books, 1963.

Choron, J. *Modern man and mortality*. New York: The Macmillan Company, 1964.

Duff, R., & Hollingshead, A. *Sickness and society*. New York, Ebbingsdon, and London: Harper and Row, 1968.

Feifel, H. (Ed.) *The meaning of death*. New York: McGraw-Hill Book Company, 1959.

Fulton, R. (Ed.) *Death and identity*. New York: Wiley and Sons, 1965.

Resnik, H. L. P. (Ed.) *Suicidal behaviors: Diagnosis and management*. Boston: Little, Brown and Company, 1968.

Kubler-Ross, E. *On death and dying*. New York: The Macmillan Company, 1969.

Schoenberg, B., Carr, A., Peretz, D., & Kutscher, A. (Eds.) *Loss and grief: Psychological management in medical practice*. New York: Columbia University Press, 1970.

Shneidman, E. S. (Ed.) *Essays in self-destruction*. New York: Science House, 1967.

Toynbee, A., et al. *Man's concern with death*. St. Louis, New York, and San Francisco: McGraw-Hill Book Company, 1968.

Vernick, J. *Selected bibliography on death and dying*. Washington, D.C.: Information Office, National Institute of Child Health and Human Development, U.S. Department of Health, Education, and Welfare, 1971.

Weber, F. *Aspects of death and correlated aspects of life in art, epigram, and poetry: Contributions towards an anthology and an iconography*. (4th ed.) London: H. K. Lewis and Company, Ltd., 1922.

227

Chapter 1 The Practical Significance of Mortality

Abrahamsson, H. *The origin of death: Studies in African mythology*. Uppsala: (Studia ethnographica Upsaliensia, 3), 1951.

Blauner, R. Death and social structure. *Psychiatry*, 1966, 29, 378-394.

Comper, F. (Ed.) *The book of the craft of dying, and other early English tracts concerning death*. London, New York, Bombay, and Calcutta: Longmans, Green and Company, 1917.

Eliade, M. *Shamanism: Archaic techniques of ecstasy*. (Translated by W. Trask) New York: Pantheon Books, 1964.

Frankl, V. *Man's search for meaning: An introduction to logotherapy*. New York: Washington Square Press, Inc., 1963.

Frazer, J. *The golden bough: A study in magic and religion*. (Abridged ed.) New York: The Macmillan Company, 1923.

Gorer, G. The pornography of death. In W. Phillips and P. Rahv (Eds.), *Modern writing*. New York: Berkeley, 1956.

Herberg, W. (Ed.) *Four existentialist theologians: A reader from the works of Jacques Maritain, Nicolas Berdyaev, Martin Buber, and Paul Tillich*. Garden City: Doubleday Anchor Books, 1958.

Lifton, R. *Death in life: Survivors of Hiroshima*. New York: Random House, 1967.

Niederland, W. The problem of the survivor. Part I. Some remarks on the psychiatric evaluation of emotional disorders in survivors of Nazi persecution. *Journal of Hillside Hospital*, 1961, 10, 233-247.

Niederland, W. The problem of the survivor. In H. Kyrstal (Ed.), *Massive psychic trauma*. New York: International Universities Press, Inc., 1968.

Osler, W. *Science and immortality. The Ingersoll lecture, 1904*. Cambridge: Houghton Mifflin & Co., Riverside Press, 1904.

Rivers, W. H. R. The primitive conception of death. In *Psychology and ethnology*. London: Kegan, Paul, Trench, Trubner, 1926.

Weisman, A. D. Birth of the death people. *Omega: Newsletter of Time, Perspective, Death and Bereavement*, 1, 1967, 1.

Werner, H. *Comparative psychology of human development*. (Rev. ed.) New York: International Universities Press, Inc., 1957.

Additional References:

Charles, R. *Eschatology: The doctrine of a future life in Israel, Judaism, and Christianity*. New York: Schocken Books, 1963.

Steiner, F. *Taboo*. Baltimore: Penguin Books, Inc., 1967.

Chapter 2 Basic Concepts and Assumptions

Freud, S. Thoughts for the times on war and death. In *Collected papers IV*. London: Hogarth Press, 1925.

Glaser, B., & Strauss, A. *Time for dying*. Chicago: Aldine Publishing Co., 1968.

Litin, E., Rynearson, E., & Hallenbech, G. "Symposium: What shall we tell the cancer patient?" *Proceedings of the Staff Meetings of the Mayo Clinic*, 1960, 35, 10.

May, R. *The meaning of anxiety*. New York: Ronald Press, 1950.

Rheingold, J. *The mother, anxiety, and death: The catastrophic death complex.* Boston: Little, Brown and Co., 1967.

Schur, M. The ego in anxiety. In R. Loewenstein (Ed.), *Drives, affects, behavior*. New York: International Universities Press, Inc., 1953.

Schur, M. The ego and the id in anxiety. In *The psychoanalytic study of the child*. Vol. 13. New York: International Universities Press, 1958.

Weisman, A. D. The patient with a fatal illness—To tell or not to tell. *Journal of the American Medical Association*, 1967, 201, 646-648.

Additional References:

Kelly, W. D., & Friesen, S. R. Do cancer patients want to be told? *Surgery*, 1950, 27, 822-826.

Chapter 3 Common Misconceptions about Death and Denial

Campbell, P. Suicide among cancer patients. *Connecticut Health Bulletin*, 1966, 80:(9), 207-212.

Engel, G. L. A psychological setting of somatic disease: The 'giving up—given up' complex. *Proceedings of the Royal Society of Medicine*, 1967, 60, 553-555.

Engel, G. L. A life setting conducive to illness: The 'giving up—given up' complex. *Annals of Internal Medicine*, 1968, 69, 293-300.

Farberow, N., Shneidman, E., and Leonard, C.: Suicide among General Medical and Surgical Hospital Patients with Malignant Neoplasms, *Veterans Administration Medical Bulletin*, 9 (1963), 1-11.

Menninger, K. *Man against himself*. New York: Harcourt, Brace and Co., 1938.

Parkes, C. M. The first year of bereavement: A longitudinal study of the reaction of London widows to the death of their husbands. *Psychiatry*, 1970, 33:(4), 444-467.

Saul, L. J. Sudden death at impasse. *Psychoanalytic Forum*, 1966, 1:(1), 88-89.

Schmale, A. A genetic view of affects: With special reference to the genesis of helplessness and hopelessness. In *The psychoanalytic study of the child*. Vol. 19. New York: International Universities Press, Inc., 1964.

Sheps, J. Management of fear of death in chronic disease. *Journal of the American Geriatrics Society*, 1957, 5, 793-797.

Weisman, A. D. Misgivings and misconceptions in the psychiatric care of terminal patients. *Psychiatry*, 1970, 33:(1), 67-81.

Weisman, A. D., & Hackett, T. P. Predilection to death. *Psychosomatic Medicine*, 1961, 23, 232-255.

Additional References:

Bulger, R. J. Doctors and dying. *Archives of Internal Medicine*, 1963, 112, 327-332.

Lasagna, L. Physicians' behavior toward the dying patient. In O. Brim et al., *The dying patient*. New York: Russell Sage Foundation, 1970.

Chapter 4   Case Material and Methods

Hackett, T., & Weisman, A. D. Psychiatric management of operative syndromes: I. The therapeutic consultation and the effect of noninterpretive intervention. *Psychosomatic Medicine*, 1960, 22, 267-282.

Hackett, T., & Weisman, A. D. Psychiatric management of operative syndromes: II. Psychodynamic factors in formulation and management. *Psychosomatic Medicine*, 1960, 22, 356-372.

Weisman, A. D. The psychotherapeutic 'encounter' and clinical research. In *Proceedings of the 3rd World Congress of Psychiatry*. Montreal: McGill University Press, 1961.

Weisman, A. D., & Hackett, T. P. The dying patient. *Special Treatment Situations* (Des Plaines, Ill.: Forest Hospital Publications), 1962, 1, 16-21.

Additional References:

Eissler, K. R. *The psychiatrist and the dying patient*. New York: International Universities Press, 1955.

LeShan, L., & LeShan, E. Psychotherapy and the patient with a limited life span. *Psychiatry*, 1961, 24:(4), 318-323.

✓Verwoerdt, A. *Communication with the fatally ill*. Springfield, Ill.: Charles C. Thomas, 1966.

Chapter 5   Denial and Middle Knowledge

Fenichel, O. *The psychoanalytic theory of neurosis*. New York: W. W. Norton and Company, 1945.

Freud, A. *The ego and the mechanisms of defence.* (Translated by C. Baines) London: Hogarth Press, Ltd. and the Institute of Psycho-Analysis, 1948.

Lewin, B. *The psychoanalysis of elation.* New York: W. W. Norton and Company, 1950.

Rosen, J., & Bibring, G. Psychological reactions of hospitalized male patients to a heart attack: Age and social-class differences. *Psychosomatic Medicine*, 1966, 28, 808-821.

Weisman, A. D., & Hackett, T. P. Denial as a social act. In S. Levin and R. Kahana (Eds.), *Psychodynamic studies on aging: Creativity, reminiscing, and dying.* New York: International Universities Press, 1967.

Additional References:

Leveton, A. Time, death, and the ego-chill. *Journal of Existentialism*, 1965, 6, 69-80.

Levin, R. Truth versus illusion in relation to death. *Psychoanalytic Review*, 1964, 51, 22-32.

Parsons, T., & Lidz, V. Death in American society. In E. S. Shneidman (Ed.), *Essays in self-destruction.* New York: Science House, 1967.

Shneidman, E. S. Orientations toward death: A vital aspect of the study of lives. In R. W. White (Ed.), *The study of lives.* New York: Atherton Press, 1963.

Chapter 6 Denial and Acceptance in Myocardial Infarction and Cancer

Feder, S. Psychological considerations in the care of patients with cancer. In C. Bahnson and D. Kissen (Eds.), *Psychophysiological aspects of cancer. Annals of New York Academy of Sciences*, 1966, 125, 1020-1027.

Hackett, T., & Weisman, A. D. Denial as a factor in patients with heart disease and cancer. In L. White (Ed.), *Care of patients with fatal illness. Annals of New York Academy of Sciences*, 1969, 164, 802-817.

Oken, D. What to tell cancer patients: A study of medical attitudes. *Journal of the American Medical Association*, 1961, 175:(13), 1120-1128.

Rothenberg, A. Psychological problems in terminal cancer management. *Cancer*, 1961, 14, 1063-1073.

Waxenberg, S. The importance of the communication of feelings about cancer. In C. Bahnson and D. Kissen (Eds.), *Psychophysiological aspects of cancer. Annals of New York Academy of Sciences*, 1966, 125, 1000-1005.

Additional References:

Cassem, N. H., Wishnie, H. A., & Hackett, T. P. How coronary patients respond to last rites. *Postgraduate Medicine*, 1969, 45, 147-152.

Druss, R. G., & Kornfeld, D. S. The survivors of cardiac arrest: A psychiatric study. *Journal of the American Medical Association*, 1967, **201**, 291-296.

Friedman, M., & Rosenman, R. Association of specific overt behavior patterns with blood and cardiovascular findings: Blood cholesterol level, blood clotting time, incidence of Arcus Senilis, and clinical coronary artery disease. *Journal of the American Medical Association*, 1959, **169**, 1286-1296.

Hackett, T. P., Cassem, N. H., & Wishnie, H. A. The coronary-care unit: An appraisal of its psychological hazards. *New England Journal of Medicine*, 1968, **279**, 1365-1370.

Chapter 7 Death from a Fatal Illness: Cancer

Aitken-Swan, J., & Easson, E. C. Reactions of cancer patients on being told their diagnosis. *British Medical Journal*, 1959, **1**, 779-783.

Goldsen, R. K. Patient delay in seeking cancer diagnosis: Behavioral aspects. *Journal of Chronic Diseases*, 1963, **16**, 427.

Lynch, H. T., & Krush, A. J. Attitudes and delay in cancer detection. *Cancer: Journal for Clinicians*, 1968, **18**, 287-293.

Moses, R., & Cividali, N. Differential levels of awareness of illness: Their relation to some salient features in cancer patients. In C. Bahnson and D. Kissen (Eds.), *Psychophysiological aspects of cancer. Annals of New York Academy of Sciences*, 1966, **125**, 984-994.

Sutherland, R. *Cancer: The significance of delay*. London: Butterworth and Company, Ltd., 1960.

Weisman, A. D., & Worden, J. J. W. Social significance of the danger list. *Journal of the American Medical Association*, 1971, **215**:(12), 1963-1966.

Additional References:

Abrams, R. D. The cancer patient, his changing pattern of communication. *New England Journal of Medicine*, 1966, **274**, 397-322.

Bahnson, C., & Kissen, D. (Eds.) *Psychophysiological aspects of cancer. Annals of New York Academy of Sciences*, 1966, **125**, 733-1055.

Hackett, T. P., & Weisman, A. D. Human reactions to the imminence of death. In H. Wechsler and M. Greenblatt (Eds.), *The threat of impending disaster*. Cambridge: M.I.T. Press, 1964.

LeShan, L. Cancer mortality rate: Some statistical evidence of the effect of psychological factors. *Archives of General Psychiatry*, 1962, **6**, 333-335.

Chapter 8 The Terminal Stage

Norton, J. Treatment of a dying patient. In *The psychoanalytic study of the child*. Vol. 18. New York: International Universities Press, Inc., 1963.

Reed, A. W. Problems of impending death: The concerns of the dying patient. *Journal of the American Physical Therapy Association*, 1968, 48, 740-742.

Saunders, C. The treatment of intractable pain in terminal cancer. *Proceedings of the Royal Society of Medicine*, 1963, 56:(3), 195-197.

Saunders, C. The last stages of life. *American Journal of Nursing*, 1965, 65, 70-75.

Additional References:

Aldrich, C. K. The dying patient's grief. *Journal of the American Medical Association*, 1963, 184, 329-331.

Gengerelli, J. A., & Kirkner, F. J. (Eds.) *Psychological factors in human cancer*. Berkeley: University of California Press, 1953.

Gerle, B., Lunden, G., & Sandblom, P. The patient with inoperable cancer from the psychiatric and social standpoints: A study of 101 cases. *Cancer*, 1960, 13, 1206-1217.

Hackett, T. P., & Weisman, A. D. The treatment of the dying. *Current Psychiatric Therapies*, 1962, 2, 121-126.

Kazzaz, D. and Vickers, R. Geriatric Staff Attitudes towards Death, *Journal of American Geriatrics Society*, 16 (1968), 1364-1374.

LeShan, L. L., & Reznikoff, M. Psychosomatic aspects of cancer. *Psychosomatic Medicine*, 1961, 23, 258-262.

Stavraky, K., et al. Psychological factors in the outcome of human cancer. *Journal of Psychosomatic Research*, 1968, 12:(4), 251-259.

Chapter 9 Death from Terminal Old Age

Aldrich, C. K., & Mendkoff, E. Relocation of the aged and disabled: A mortality study. *Journal of the American Geriatrics Society*, 1963, 11, 185-194.

Brill, N. Basic knowledge for work with aging. *The Gerontologist*, 1969, 9:(3), 197-203.

Butler, R. The destiny of creativity in later life: Studies of creative people and the creative process. In R. Kahana and S. Levin (Eds.), *Psychodynamic studies on aging: Creativity, reminiscing, and dying*. New York: International Universities Press, Inc., 1967.

Erikson, E. Eight ages of man. *International Journal of Psychiatry*, 1966, 2, 281-307.

Feifel, H. Older persons look at death. *Geriatrics*, 1956, 11, 127-130.

Hollingshead, A., & Redlich, F. *Social class and mental illness: A community study*. New York: Science Editions, John Wiley and Sons, Inc., 1958.

Kastenbaum, R. (Ed.) *New thoughts on old age*. New York: Springer Publishing Company, Inc., 1964.

Lieberman, M. A. Relationship of mortality rates to entrance to a home for the aged. *Geriatrics*, 1961, 16, 515-519.

Lowenthal, M. Some social dimensions of psychiatric disorders in old age. In *Processes of aging: Social and psychological perspectives*. Vol. 2. New York: Atherton Press, 1963.

Maslow, A. A theory of metamotivation: The biological rooting of the value-life. *Journal of Humanistic Psychology*, 1967, 7, 93-127.

Sachs, H. In A. Roback (Ed.), *The creative unconscious: Studies in the psychoanalysis of art*. (2nd ed.) Cambridge: Science-Art Publishers, 1951.

Shneidman, E. Suicide, lethality, and the psychological autopsy. In E. Shneidman and M. Ortega (Eds.), *Aspects of Depression, International Psychiatry Clinics*. Vol. 6, No. 2. Boston: Little, Brown and Company, 1969.

Simmons, L. W. *Role of the aged in primitive society*. New Haven: Yale University Press, 1945.

Sudnow, D. *Passing on: The social organization of dying*. Englewood Cliffs, New Jersey: Prentice Hall, 1967.

Weisman, A. D., & Kastenbaum, R. *The psychological autopsy: A study of the terminal phase of life*. New York: Community Mental Health Monographs, No. 4, 1968.

Williams, R., Tibbitts, C., & Donahue, W. (Eds.) *Processes of aging: Social and psychological perspectives*. (2 vols.) New York: Atherton Press, 1963.

Additional References:

Cumming, E., & Henry, W. *Growing old: A view in depth of the social and psychological processes in aging*. New York: Basic Books, 1961.

Lipowski, A. J. Psychosocial aspects of disease. *Annals of Internal Medicine*, 1969, 71:(6), 1197-1206.

Zinker, J., & Fink, S. The possibility for psychological growth in a dying person. *Journal of General Psychology*, 1966, 74, 185-199.

Chapter 10 Indications of Impending Death

Abram, H. S. Adaption to open heart surgery: A psychiatric study of response to the threat of death. *American Journal of Psychiatry*, 1965, 122, 659-667.

Ayd, F. J., Jr. The hopeless case: Medical and moral considerations. *Journal of the American Medical Association*, 1962, 181, 1099-1102.

Burrell, R. J. W. in Spells, sorcery and the will to die. *Medical World News*, 1961, II:(25), 33-34.

Camus, A. *The Plague*. (Translated by S. Gilbert) New York: Modern Library, 1948.

Feinstein, A. A new staging system for cancer and reappraisal of 'early' treatment and 'cure' by radical surgery. *New England Journal of Medicine*, 1968, **279**, 747-753.

Glaser, B. G., & Strauss, A. L. Awareness contexts and social interaction. *American Sociological Review*, 1964, **29**, 669-679.

Hilgard, J. Depressive and psychotic states as anniversaries to sibling death in childhood. In E. Shneidman and M. Ortega (Eds.), *Aspects of depression, International Psychiatry Clinics*. Vol. 6, No. 2. Boston: Little, Brown and Company, 1961.

Lieberman, M. A. Observations on death and dying. *Gerontologist*, 1966, **6**, 70-72.

Leiberman, M. A., & Coplan, A. S. Distance from death as a variable in the study of aging. *Developmental Psychology*, 1970, **2**:(1), 71-84.

Mann, T. *Death in Venice and seven other stories*. (Translated by H. Lowe-Porter) New York: Vintage Books, Random House, 1936.

Thomas, B. *King Cohn: The life and times of Harry Cohn*. New York: Bantam Books, 1968.

Von Lerchenthal, E. M. Death from psychic causes. *Bulletin of the Menninger Clinic*, 1948, **12**, 31-36.

Wilson, I. C., & Reece, J. C. Simultaneous death in schizophrenic twins. *Archives of General Psychiatry*, 1964, **11**, 377-384.

Zinsser, H. *As I remember him: The biography of R. S.* Boston: Little, Brown, and Company, 1940.

Additional References:

Barber, T. X. Death by suggestion: A critical note. *Psychosomatic Medicine*, 1961, **23**, 153-155.

Barrett, G. V., & Franke, R. H. 'Psychogenic' death: A reappraisal. *Science*, 1970, **167**:(3916), 304-306.

Crawford, J. R. *Witchcraft and sorcery in Rhodesia*. London: Oxford University Press, 1967.

Lion, J. R., & Hackett, T. P. Forewarnings of illness: Predictions and premonitions in cancer patients. *American Journal of Psychiatry*, 1968, **125**, 137-140.

Raybin, J. The curse: A study in family communication. *American Journal of Psychiatry*, 1970, **127**:(5), 617-625.

Schmidt, B., & Schmidt, J. Psychological death in headshrinkers. *American Journal of Psychiatry*, 1964, **121**, 510-511.

Tinling, D. Voodoo, root work, and medicine. *Psychosomatic Medicine*, 1967, **29**, 483-490.

Chapter 11 Counterparts of Death

Alexander, I. E., & Adlerstein, A. M. Studies in the psychology of death. In H. P. David and J. C. Brenglemann, (Eds.), *Perspectives in personality research*. New York: Springer, 1960; 65-92.

Beigler, J. S. Anxiety as an aid in the prognostication of impending death. *American Medical Association Archives of Neurology and Psychology*, 1957, 77, 171-177.

Herzog, E. *Psyche and death*. (Translated by B. Cox and E. Rolfe) London: Hodger and Stoughton, Ltd., 1966.

Le Comte, E. (Ed.) *Dictionary of last words*. New York: Philosophical Library, 1955.

Pelgrin, M. In S. Moon and E. Howes (Eds.), *And a time to die*. London: Routledge and Kegan Paul, 1961.

Ryle, J. A. The sense of dying. *Guy's Hospital Reports*, 1950, 99, 223-235.

Additional References:

Forest, J. D. The major emphasis of the funeral. *Pastoral Psychology*, 1963, 14:(135), 19-24.

Hall, G. S. Thanatophobia and immortality. *American Journal of Psychology*, 1915, 26, 550-613.

Rosenthal, H. R. The fear of death as an indispensable factor in psychotherapy. *American Journal of Psychotherapy*, 1963, 17, 619-630.

Ulanov, B. *Death: A book of preparation and consolation*. New York: Sheed and Ward, 1959.

Zilboorg, G. Fear of death. *Psychoanalytic Quarterly*, 1943, 12, 465-475.

Chapter 12 Death and Responsibility

Weisman, A. *The existential core of psychoanalysis: Reality sense and responsibility*. Boston: Little, Brown and Company, 1965.

Weisman, A. Death and responsibility: A psychiatrist's view. *Psychiatric Opinion*, 1966, 3, 22-26.

Additional References:

Ackerknecht, E. H. Death in the history of medicine. *Bulletin of the History of Medicine*, 1968, 42, 19-23.

Diggory, J. C. The components of personal despair. In E. S. Shneidman (Ed.), *Essays in self-destruction*. New York: Science House, 1967.

Hinton, J. M. The physical and mental distress of the dying. *Quarterly Journal of Medicine*, 1963, New Series, **32**:(126), 1-21.

Kaufmann, W. Existentialiam and death. In H. Feifel (Ed.), *The meaning of death*. New York: McGraw-Hill, 1959.

Lasagna, L. The doctor and the dying patient. *Journal of Chronic Diseases*, 1969, **22**:(2), 65-68.

Pattison, E. M. On the failure to forgive or to be forgiven. *American Journal of Psychotherapy*, 1965, **19**:(1), 106-115.

Pattison, E. M. The experience of dying. *American Journal of Psychotherapy*, 1967, **21**:(1), 32-43.

Taylor, J. *The rule and exercises of holy dying*. London: Bell and Daldy, Fleet St., 1857.

Worcester, A. *The care of the aged, the dying, and the dead*. Springfield, Ill.: Charles C Thomas, 1940.

Chapter 13 Illusion and Incipient Death

Camus, A. *The myth of Sisyphus and other essays*. (Translated by J. O'Brien) New York: Alfred A. Knopf, 1955.

Freud, S. *The future of an illusion*, 1927. (Translated by J. Strachey) *Standard edition of complete psychological works*, Vol. 21. London: Hogarth Press and Institute of Psycho-Analysis, 1961.

Weisman, A. D. Reality sense and reality testing. *Behavioral Science*, 1958, 3, 228-261.

Additional References:

Bell, T. *In the midst of life*. New York: Atheneum, 1961.

Fraser, J. T. (Ed.) *The voices of time: A cooperative survey of man's view of time as expressed by the sciences and by the humanities*. New York: George Braziller, 1966.

Glaser, B., & Strauss, A. *Awareness of dying*. Chicago: Aldine Publishing Company, 1965.

Kastenbaum, R. On the meaning of time in later life. *Journal of Genetic Psychology*, 1966, **109**, 9-25.

Landsberg, P. L. *The experience of death: The moral problem of suicide*. New York: Philosophical Library, 1953.

Richardson, W. *Heidegger: Through phenomenology to thought*. The Hague: Martinus Nijhoff, 1963.

Schur, M. The problem of death in Freud's writings and life. New York: 14th Freud Anniversary Lecture, 1964.

Weisman, A. D. The right way to die. *Psychiatric and Social Science Review*, 1968, **2**, 2-7.

Index

239